CHARLTON HESTON

PRESENTS

THE BIBLE

CHARLTON HESTON

presents

The BIBLE

GT Publishing
New York
1997

FRONTISPIECE: *Charlton Heston in Jerusalem. The gold dome in the background is part of the Mosque of the Dome of the Rock.*

Additional acknowledgments and picture credits are on page 288
Developed by Robotham Associates, Inc., Norfolk, Virginia
Biblical text redactions by Charlton Heston
Commentaries by Charlton Heston and Tom Robotham
Maps by Pantheon Produtions, Inc.
Photographs by Frank Micelotta
Based on the Agamemnon Films Production CHARLTON HESTON PRESENTS THE BIBLE
Executive Producers: Fraser C. Heston and Philip D. Fehrle
Produced by John Stronach and Gwen Field
Directed by Tony Westman

SPECIAL THANKS TO JOHN STRONACH, CAROL LANNING AND THE REV. JAMES HUTTON.

Published in 1997 by GT Publishing Corporation
16 East 40th Street
New York, NY 10016

Library of Congress Cataloging-in-Publication Data
Bible. English. Authorized. Selection. 1997.
Charlton Heston Presents the Bible: a companion for families.
p. cm.
Includes index.
ISBN 1-55719-270-2 (hardcover)
I. Heston, Charlton. II. Title.
BS391.2.H46 1997
22.5'2034—dc21   97-28438
                                                  CIP
ISBN: 1-57719-270-2

Printed in Canada
10 9 8 7 6 5 4 3 2
Second printing

Table of Contents

Charlton Heston inside the ruins of a first-century Roman amphitheater in Israel.

Preface

To call the Bible a great book is an understatement. It is, quite simply, the cornerstone of Western Civilization. In its two testaments, it stands as law and scripture for two of the great religions of the world. And it shares with a third, the Muslim faith, several of its significant figures and stories. But the Bible's reach extends beyond the realm of religion. As a work of literature, it has had an immeasurable impact on our greatest writers, artists and composers—and thus, on our culture as a whole. Directly and indirectly, it has shaped our ideas about good and evil, loyalty and betrayal, hope and despair, love and hate, and the meaning of life itself.

How did this happen? How did the Bible become what it is today? To some extent, the origins of the Scriptures remain shrouded in mystery. But one thing is clear: the stories in the Bible emerged from ancient oral traditions. The prophets and holy men who roamed the Middle East seeking the truth, and preaching God's word as they perceived it, were talking to illiterate audiences who could only be reached by the witnessed testimony of the spoken word. Their exhortations, their songs and parables—the testament

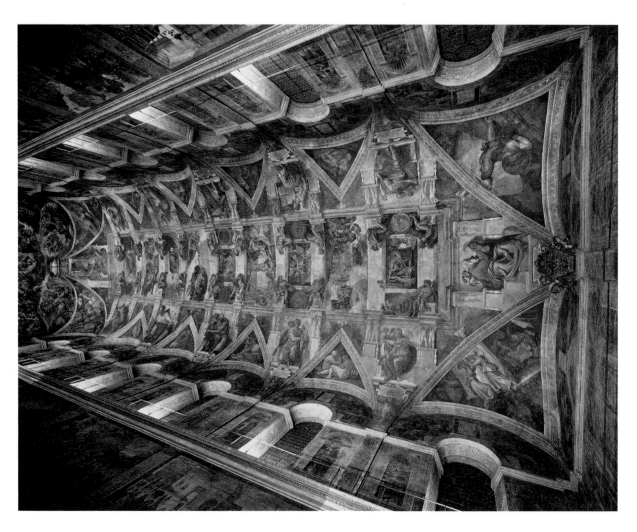

Overview of Michelangelo's monumental work on the ceiling of the Sistine Chapel.

of faith they offered—were preserved and passed on from generation to generation, through the telling of stories.

In the case of the Old Testament, these tale-tellers carried their message centuries before the Phoenicians invented writing. Each of them would have to recruit his own replacement—a 12-year-old orphan, most likely. "All right, boy, you listen now. I'll watch over you, give you a safe place to sleep, but you have to sit by the fire every night when I tell these stories. You have to listen and learn them, by heart. When I'm gone, you have to become the tale-teller."

That's where I come in. I'm not a priest or a scholar. I'm a storyteller. And as such, I have always been fascinated by the books of the Bible, in both testaments. There simply are no greater stories to tell.

When Mr. DeMille cast me as Moses in the movie *The Ten Commandments*, in the summer of 1954, I well understood the problems facing me in the months before we began filming on the Red Sea, Mount Sinai and the Egyptian desert. Not just the endless wardrobe fittings (women love wardrobe fittings, men hate them) and the makeup tests (I had 11 different makeups in that film) but the far more important task of researching the man himself.

Moses. Surely he is one of the great figures in world history. As I soon

Jerusalem's Western Wall, also known as the "Wailing Wall," where devout Jews still come to pray.

discovered, there are more books about Moses than anyone except Jesus. He is revered by three of the world's great religions, though none calls him divine. He was a man, and flawed, as all of us are. He led his rebellious people through 40 years of wandering in the desert, yet God denied him the triumph of leading them "over Jordan!!" Still, "There arose not a prophet since in Israel like Moses, whom the Lord knew . . . face to face."

I read as many of the multitude of books on Moses as I could, from Breasted's *History of Egypt* to Sigmund Freud's *Moses and Monotheism.* All

ABOVE: *Charlton Heston as Moses, in the movie* The Ten Commandments.

OPPOSITE: *Moses, Tomb of Pope Julius II.* Michelangelo Buonarroti. Vatican.

taught me a great deal—though none all I needed, of course.

After the year we spent shooting the film, I realized more and more the power of the texts themselves, explored simply as great stories rather than as fragments that Mr. DeMille had used for his film. He'd commissioned a massive research project, extending over several years, without which the picture couldn't have been made. But few of the actual lines from the Five Books of Moses were spoken on the screen. For that matter, rabbis, priests and ministers often use no more than a verse or two from the Bible during religious services, and when they do so, it is generally as a preface to their sermons and

The summit of Mount Sinai. It is here that Moses is said to have received the Tablets of Law from God.

lessons. I don't mean to suggest that there is anything wrong with that. My point is, simply, that people are not exposed to the Bible to the degree that they once were.

Over the years, I found myself more and more often *performing* Biblical stories—the death of Moses, the Crucifixion, the Flood—in various live venues, with enormous success. Several years ago, I decided to explore the Bible in greater depth than I had before. The result of this exploration led to a successful television series. The series, which was later adapted for videotape and CD-ROM, was called, "Charlton Heston Presents The Bible." In the course of the programs, I took viewers on a journey through the Holy Land. We toured ancient sites, from the banks of the Jordan to the top of Mount Sinai and explored the relationship between Scripture and history. I also offered readings of my favorite stories and illustrated them with great works of art.

Reading these stories aloud is important. As I have noted, the Biblical stories were originally passed on by word of mouth. Even in the time of Christ—several thousand years after the time of the great Hebrew patriarchs—most people were illiterate. Thus the evangelists would have wandered through the countryside, assembling random audiences of perhaps a dozen fishermen, shepherds or shopkeepers: "Listen to me, now. This is what He did; this is what He said. Believe me . . . I was THERE."

I'm convinced that the narrative power of these stories in both testaments depends partly on the fact that they were all developed orally. That's why

Crossing the Red Sea.

they're so powerful when spoken. Go ahead, try it yourself. Read one of the stories we've printed in this book to your family and see how exciting it is—how easy it is to follow. Take the first words in the Bible, if you like:

In the Beginning, God created the Heavens and the Earth.

The Earth was without form, and void . . . the darkness was over all. Then the spirit of God moved upon the face of the deep. God said, "Let there be light!"

And there was light.

When you read these words out loud, I think you'll agree that doing so is a wonderful way to experience their power. That, ultimately, is why I did the television series. Film, after all, is a wonderful medium. It can capture the energy of the live performance and transmit it to people who would not otherwise be able to experience it. But film also has its drawbacks. It does not allow time for reflection—time to focus on the subtleties of an especially beautiful phrase or visual rendering.

This book, which is based on the television series, allows you to do just that. It is my hope that you will find it useful. We're calling it "a companion for families" because we believe that children and adults alike will find it accessible. In addition to reproductions of classic paintings, and photographs taken on location during the production of the television series, you'll find my own redactions of Biblical stories. The redactions closely follow the King James Bible because I share with many people the belief that this version is a monument to English prose. (It has also been called "the only great work of art ever created by a committee" because it took 47 scholars some *seven years* to translate it.)

Many people imagine the King James version to be filled with difficult language. Admittedly, parts of it do sound strange to the modern ear. But much of it is simple and clear. And taken as a whole, it is undeniably a great piece of writing.

To help you put the Biblical stories in perspective, I have included brief commentaries in each chapter. You'll also find a few reference sections in the back of the book: a book-by-book summary of the Bible, a who's who and suggestions for further reading.

As I noted before, I am not a scholar. In producing the commentaries, I have drawn on the works of scholars, and I remain forever indebted to them. But this is not a work of scholarship. It's a series of personal impressions— a record, if you will, of my own exhilarating efforts to understand this majestic body of work. If, in sharing my thoughts, I can help you and your family achieve a deeper appreciation of the Bible, then I will consider this endeavor to have been worthwhile.

Peace be with you.

Charlton Heston

OPPOSITE: *The Lindisfarne Gospels, St. Matthew.*

imagohominis

DACTI
HAT
heus

Creation of the Sun, Moon and Planets. 1509-1512. Michelangelo Buonarroti. Sistine Chapel, Vatican.

chapter 1

In the Beginning...

How was the universe created? Great thinkers throughout history have wrestled with this question. Today, most scientists believe it happened with a "Big Bang"—an explosion of unimaginable magnitude that left billions of star systems in its wake. But that theory raises other questions. What *caused* the explosion? And what sparked the creation of life on earth?

In the Book of *Genesis,* the answers are clear. "God created the heavens and the earth," and all the living creatures, on land and sea. Then, on the sixth day, he created man—in his own image.

This Biblical story of creation is remarkably simple. And yet, it is one of the most powerful stories in world literature. In a tone that is both straightforward and majestic, it penetrates to the very core of our being and appeals to our fundamental yearning to understand the ultimate source of life.

Scientists, undoubtedly, will continue to search for clues that might explain the essence of the universe. But as long as our origins remain shrouded in mystery, the opening stories of the book of *Genesis* will resonate within our souls.

Separation of Earth and Water. 1509-1512. Michelangelo Buonarroti. Sistine Chapel, Vatican.

Creation

In the beginning, God created the heavens and the earth. The earth was without form, and void; the darkness was over all.

Then the spirit of God moved upon the face of the deep. God said, "Let there be light!". . . and there was light. And God saw the light, that it was good; so He

Adam and Eve. c. 1528. Lucas Cranach, the Elder.
Courtald Institute Galleries.

divided the light from the darkness. God called the light Day, and the darkness He called Night. And the evening and the morning were the first day.

Now God said, "Let there be a firmament in the midst of the waters, and let it divide the waters from the waters." And it was so. God called the firmament Heaven. And the evening and the morning were the second day.

Then God said, "Let the waters under heaven be gathered together and let the dry land appear." And it was so. God called the dry land Earth; the gathering together of the waters He called Seas; and He saw that it was good. So God said, "Let the earth bring forth grass, and trees yielding fruit, each after its own kind." And it was so. God saw that it was good. And the evening and the morning were the third day.

Then God said, "Let there be lights in the firmament of heaven to divide the day from the night. Let them be for signs, to mark the seasons, the days, and the years. Let them be to give light upon the earth."

And it was so. God made two great lights; the greater light to rule the day, the lesser light to rule the night. He made the stars also and set them in the firmament of heaven to divide the day from the night. And God saw that it was good, and the evening and the morning were the fourth day.

Then God said, "Let the waters bring forth abundantly moving creatures that have life, and fowl that may fly above the earth in the open firmament of heaven." And He created great whales, and every living creature that moveth in the waters after their kind, and every winged fowl after its kind. And God saw that it was good. And the evening and the morning were the fifth day.

Now God said, "Let the earth bring forth living creatures, the beasts of the earth." And it was so. God made the beasts, each after his kind; cattle and everything that

moves upon the earth; and God saw that it was good.

So at last God said, "Let us make man in our own image, after our likeness, and let him have dominion over all the earth." So the Lord God formed man out of the dust of the ground, and breathed into his nostrils the breath of life, and man became a living soul.

God blessed him and said, "Be fruitful and multiply, and replenish the earth, and subdue it; and have dominion over the fish of the sea, and over the fowl of the air, and over every living thing that moveth upon the earth."

But then God said, "Behold, I have given you every plant bearing seed upon the face of all the earth, and every tree in which there is fruit; to you it shall be for food. And so, to every beast of the earth, to every fowl of the air, to all upon the earth wherein there is life, I

ABOVE: *Creation of the Animals.*
Flemish School.
Pamplona Museum.

OVERLEAF: *Creation of Adam.*
1509-1512. Michelangelo
Buonarroti. Sistine Chapel,
Vatican.

give every green thing for food." And it was so.

Then, God saw everything that He had made, and behold, it was very good. And the evening and the morning were the sixth day. Thus the heavens and the earth were finished, all the host of them. So on the seventh day, God ended His work which He had made. And He rested.

The Garden of Eden

Then he planted a garden eastward in Eden, and there he put the man he had formed. And he called him Adam.

He put him into the garden to till it and to keep it, and out of the ground the Lord God made every tree grow that is pleasant to the sight, and good for food; the tree of Life also in the midst of the garden and the tree of knowledge of good and evil.

And the Lord God commanded the man saying, "Of every tree of the garden thou mayest freely eat. But of the tree of the knowledge of good and evil, thou shalt not eat of it; for in the day that thou eatest thereof thou shalt surely die."

Now the Lord God had formed every beast of the field, and every fowl of the air, so He brought them to Adam to see what he would call them; and whatsoever Adam called every living creature, that was the name thereof. Adam gave names to all the fowl and the beasts.

Then Lord God said, "It is not good that the man should be alone. I will make him a helpmate." And God caused a deep sleep to fall upon Adam, and while he slept, God took one of Adam's ribs, and closed up the flesh thereof. And from the rib, which the Lord God had taken from man, He made a woman and brought her to the man. And Adam said, "This is now bone of my bone, and flesh of my flesh; she shall be called woman because she was taken out of man.

"Therefore shall a man leave his father and his

ABOVE: *Creation of Eve.* 1509-1512.
Michelangelo Buonarroti. Sistine Chapel, Vatican.

OVERLEAF: *Paradise.* 1615.
Peter Paul Rubens. The Hague, Mauritshuis.

mother, and shall cleave to his wife."

And they were both naked, the man and the woman, and were not ashamed.

Paradise Lost

Now the serpent was more cunning than any beast which the Lord God had made. And he said to the woman, "Yea, hath God not said, 'Ye shall eat of every tree of the garden?'"

And the woman said, "We may eat of the fruit of the trees which are in the garden, but of the fruit of the tree which is in the midst of the garden, God hath said, 'Ye shall not eat of it, neither shall ye touch it, lest ye die.'"

"Ye shall not surely die," said the serpent, "For God doth know that in the day ye eat thereof, then your eyes shall be opened, and ye shall be like God, knowing good and evil."

And when the woman saw that the tree was good for food, and pleasant to the eyes, a fruit to be desired to make one wise, she took the fruit and did eat, and gave also to her husband; and he did eat with her.

And the eyes of them both were opened, and they knew that they were naked, and so they sewed fig leaves together, and made themselves aprons.

Then they heard the voice of the Lord God walking in the garden in the cool of the day. And Adam and his wife hid themselves from the presence of God, amongst the trees of the garden. And the Lord God called to Adam, "Where art thou?"

Adam said, "I heard Thy voice in the garden, and I was afraid, because I was naked. So I hid myself."

And God said, "Who told thee that thou wast naked? Hast thou eaten of the tree, whereof I commanded thee that thou shouldest not eat?"

And Adam said, "The woman Thou made to be with me, she gave me of the tree, and I did eat."

And God said to the woman, "What is this that thou hast done?" And the woman said, "The serpent beguiled me, and I did eat."

And the Lord said to the serpent, "Because thou hast done this, thou art cursed above every beast of the field; upon thy belly shalt thou go, and dust shalt thou eat all the days of thy life; I will put enmity between thee and the woman, and between thy seed and her seed; he shall strike thy head and thou shall strike his heel."

To the woman, God said, "I will multiply thy sorrow

The Symbolism of the Serpent

The story of Adam and Eve has forever fixed in our minds the image of the serpent as a symbol of evil. But in the ancient world, the serpent was not always seen in a negative light. The Canaanites, for example, associated the serpent with fertility.

Some people also believed that snakes—while potentially deadly—had healing powers. This belief is reflected in the Bible. In the book of Numbers, *God sends "fiery serpents" to attack the Israelites in response to their expressed lack of faith. When the people realize they have sinned, God tells Moses to make a bronze serpent and sets it on a pole. He then informs Moses that anyone who is bitten can be cured by simply looking at the icon.*

The story apparently had great meaning for the early Israelites because when the Temple of Jerusalem was constructed during the reign of Solomon, a bronze serpent was placed within it.

The World was
all before them,
where to choose
Their place of
rest, and Providence
their guide:
They hand in
hand with
wand'ring steps
and slow,
Through Eden
took their solitary
way.

JOHN MILTON
Paradise Lost, Book XII

and thy conception; in sorrow shalt thou bring forth children." And to Adam, he said, "Because thou hearkened unto thy wife, and ate of the tree of which I commanded thee, 'Thou must not eat,' cursed is the ground for thy sake; in sorrow shalt thou eat of it all the days of thy life, till thou return into the ground; for out of it wast thou taken; dust thou art, and unto dust shalt thou return."

Therefore the Lord God sent them forth from the garden; He drove out the man and the woman and placed cherubims at the east of Eden and a flaming sword which always turned to keep the way of the tree of life.

And this is the book of the generations of Adam in the day that God created man in the likeness of God.

OPPOSITE: *Fall of Adam and Eve.* c. 1659. Hugo van der Goes. Kunsthistoriches Museum, Vienna.

BELOW: *Expulsion from the Garden of Eden.* c. 1840. Thomas Cole. Museum of Fine Arts, Boston.

OVERLEAF: *The Fall and Expulsion.* 1509-1512. Michelangelo Buonarroti. Sistine Chapel, Vatican.

In every culture, in every time, man has tried to capture the face of the Almighty—in paint and pencil, bronze and stone. We can't say whether anybody's gotten it right, of course. But the image of God introduced in the first chapters of *Genesis* remains incredibly vivid, even in this day and age. In these stories, God's creatures have no doubt what God looks like. He's there—part of the daily life of the man and woman He had made with His own hand.

But the intimacy between God and His people is soon disturbed. When Adam and Eve eat the apple they are transformed. They are no longer innocent children under God's protection. They have acquired God's *knowledge* of good and evil, but in the process they have become separated from God Himself. Exiled from the Garden, they and their descendants will forever be impelled to seek God and to wrestle with the mystery of creation. That has been man's most noble and frustrating occupation ever since.

The question presented by this story, of course, is whether or not God intended to create perfect beings in Adam and Eve. Perhaps He did not know what He had created and wanted to see how they would turn out. Or perhaps He knew in advance what they would do.

In the Eden story, I think God knows what will happen. Choice is the seed in the core of the fruit of knowledge. Animals move to instinct and experience, unaware of concepts of good and evil. But God made man the knowing animal who would have to learn to choose between the two.

The exhilarating idea underlying this story is that Adam and Eve have the ability to choose. The remainder of the Bible is largely an account of man's attempt to realize this potential for goodness—and of God's response to man's efforts. Repeatedly, God shows forgiveness in the face of man's failures. But at times, especially in the Old Testament, He also unleashes His all-consuming wrath.

The Deluge. 1837-1840. Francis Danby. Tate Gallery, London.

chapter 2

The Wrath of God

The Old Testament stories are filled with examples of God venting his wrath. In some cases, His anger is aimed at individuals, such as Adam and Eve, or Cain. At other times, He punishes entire populations. But always, the provocation is the same: man has sinned, and must pay the price.

Throughout the Bible, of course, we are also given evidence of God's compassion. After Cain murders Abel, God curses him—but He also sets a mark upon him to protect him from vengeful hands. Later in the book of *Genesis,* God is grieved by the wickedness of humans in general. And, for a moment at least, He is sorry that He has made them. But He finds one righteous man—Noah—and decides to spare him.

When the Flood waters finally subside, God vows that He will never again "curse the ground for man's sake," even though "the imagination of man's heart is evil from his youth." God will show His anger again, to be sure. But this is not the overpowering theme of the Bible. Psalm 103 puts it all into perspective: "The Lord is merciful and gracious, slow to anger, and abounding in mercy. He will not always strive with us, nor will he keep His anger forever."

Because she would be the mother of all living persons, Adam called his wife's name Eve. And Adam knew Eve, his wife; and she conceived and bore Cain, and said, "I have gotten a man from the Lord." And she again bore his brother Abel.

Now Abel was a keeper of sheep, but Cain was a tiller of the ground. And in time it came to pass that Cain brought of the fruit of the ground an offering unto the Lord, while Abel brought the choicest of his flock. So the Lord had respect unto Abel and to his offering; but unto Cain and his offering He had no respect.

The Body of Abel Discovered by Adam. c. 1826. William Blake. Tate Gallery, London.

Thus Cain was very wroth; his countenance fell. So the Lord said to him, "Why art thou wroth, why has thy countenance fallen? If thou doest well, shalt thou not be accepted? And if thou doest not well, sin lieth at thy door."

Now it came to pass, when they were in the fields, that Cain quarreled with Abel his brother and rose up against him and slew him. Then the Lord said to Cain, "Where is Abel thy brother?" And Cain said, "I know not; am I my brother's keeper?"

And the Lord God said, "What hast thou done? The voice of thy brother's blood cries out to me from the ground! Therefore, art thou now cursed from the earth, which hath opened her mouth to receive thy brother's blood from thy hand. Henceforth, when thou tillest the ground, it shall not yield unto thee her strength; a fugitive and a vagabond shalt thou be in the earth."

And Cain said to the Lord, "My punishment is greater than I can bear. Behold, thou hast driven me out this day; and from Thy face shall I be hid. I shall be a fugitive on the face of the earth and anyone who finds me shall slay me."

But the Lord said, "Whosoever slayeth Cain, vengeance shall be taken on him sevenfold."

And the Lord set a mark upon Cain, lest any finding him should kill him.

So Cain went out from the presence of the Lord and dwelt in the land of Nod, east of Eden.

Then Adam knew his wife again; and begat a son again in his own likeness, after his image; and called his name Seth. And Eve said, "God hath given me another seed instead of Abel, whom Cain slew."

And Adam lived many years and begat sons and daughters. So it came to pass, when men began to multiply on the face of the earth, and daughters were born unto them, that the sons of God saw the daughters of

A shepherd tends his flock near modern-day Jerusalem.

The ancient Israelites were a shepherd people. This may explain why

God, in Genesis, *accepts Abel's animal sacrifice but rejects*

Cain's offering of grain. Farming was associated with the

Canaanites, who worshipped pagan gods.

men, that they were fair; and they took them as wives. And after that, when their children were born to them, these same became mighty men, men of renown.

Then Man began to call upon the name of the Lord. And the Lord said, "My Spirit shall not always strive with man, for he also is flesh. Yet his days shall be great in the earth."

There were giants in the earth in those days.

Flight of Cain (detail). 1880. Fernand Cormon. Musée d'Orsay, Paris.

Flood Myths in Other Cultures

Stories of a great flood, or deluge, are an important part of the oral and pictorial traditions of many cultures. Moreover, as the Biblical scholar J.R. Porter has pointed out, many of these stories have the same basic elements: a god, or group of gods, decides to destroy all life on earth.

But before he does, he warns one righteous man and orders him to build a ship so that he and his family can survive the flood.

In the Babylonian epic of Gilgamesh, a man named Utnapishtim is commanded to build a boat and take on board "animals of every kind, male and female." When the flood subsides, his boat comes to rest atop Mount Nisir, which is in the same region as the mountains of Ararat.

The extraordinary parallels between the stories of Utnapishtim and Noah may be attributed, in part, to the fact that both were rooted in the cultures of ancient Mesopotamia. It is worth noting, however, that similar stories have circulated within other societies having no connection to the culture of the Middle East.

Now it came to pass that the generations of the sons of Adam multiplied and waxed fat; they rode on the high places of the Earth, and ate the increase of the fields—butter of kine and milk of sheep, with fat of lambs and rams of the breed Bashan. And they did drink the pure blood of the grape.

And they said, "Our hand is high, and the Lord has not done all this!"

But their grapes were the grapes of gall, and their wine was the wine of dragons. And at last the people had corrupted themselves. They had forgotten the God that formed them. And when the Lord saw this, He said "They are children in whom there is no faith. I will hide My face from them, and see what their end will be."

But then God looked upon the earth, and behold, it was corrupt—the earth was corrupt before God and filled with violence. And God saw that the wickedness of man was in the earth.

And it grieved Him at His heart that He had made man.

So the Lord said, "Will this people rise up and go a-whoring and forsake Me? Then My anger shall be kindled against them, and I will forsake them! I will blot man, whom I created, from the face of the earth; both man and beast, and the creeping things, and the fowls of the air; it repenteth Me that I have made them."

But Noah found grace in the eyes of the Lord. He was a just man in his generation and walked with God. And God looked upon him saying, "This man shall comfort us," and called his name "Noah!"

God said, "The end of all flesh is come before Me; for the earth is filled with violence, and My way upon the earth is corrupted. Now behold, I will destroy all, with the earth.

"But go thou; make thee an ark of gopher wood.

Garden of Earthly Delights (central panel). c. 1500. Hieronymous Bosch. Museo del Prado, Madrid.

The length of it shall be three hundred cubits, and the height of it thirty cubits. Rooms shalt thou make in the ark, and a window, and a door set in the side thereof. Tar it within and without with pitch."

Thus Noah did, according to all that God commanded him.

And the Lord said unto Noah, "For that I have seen thee righteous before Me in this generation, come thou and all thy house into the ark. For behold, I shall bring a flood of waters to destroy the breath of life under heaven. And everything that is the earth shall die.

"But with thee I will establish My covenant; thou and thy sons, and thy wife and thy sons' wives with

The Building of the Ark. Jacopo da Ponte, called Il Bassano. Musée de Marseilles.

ABOVE: *The Deluge.* c. 1516. Hans Baldung-Grien. Neue Residenz, Bamberg.

OVERLEAF: *Animals Entering the Ark.* Mid to late 16th century. Jacopo da Ponte, called Il Bassano.
Musée des Beaux-Arts, Boulogne-sur-Mer.

The Deluge. 1806. Anne-Louis Girodet Trioson. The Louvre, Paris.

thee. Now of every living thing of all flesh, two of every sort must thou bring into the ark, male and female. Fowls of the air, and every beast on the earth after his kind, two of every sort shall come with thee, to keep them alive.

"And take thou with thee of all food that is eaten. Gather it to thee; it shall be food for thee and for them. Do thou keep life upon the face of all the earth.

"For I will cause it to rain, forty days and forty nights; and every living substance that I have made will I destroy."

And Noah went in, and his sons, Shem and Ham and Japeth, and his wife, and his sons' wives with him into the ark. And beasts, and fowls, and of everything that creepeth upon the earth, there went in two by two, as God commanded Noah. Two and two of all flesh, they went in, male and female. And the Lord shut them in.

And it came to pass, after seven days, that the waters of the flood were upon the earth.

All the fountains of the great deep were broken up and the windows of heaven were opened. And the rain was upon the earth forty days and forty nights.

And the waters increased, and bore up the ark, and it was lifted as the waters prevailed, and the ark went upon the face of the waters till all the high hills under heaven were covered. Fifteen cubits upward, and the mountains were covered.

And all died that moved upon the earth . . . fowl and beast and creeping thing—and every man. All died; they were destroyed from the earth!

And Noah only remained alive, and they that were with him in the ark.

And the waters prevailed.

But God remembered Noah, and the ark: He made a wind pass over the earth. And at last the windows of heaven were stopped, and the rain restrained, and the fountains of the deep also.

The Significance of the Number Forty

The number forty is used in several Biblical stories to signify a long period of time. The best-known example is in the story of the Great Flood, which continues for forty days and forty nights. Here are a few other examples.

✳

Under the leadership of Moses, the people of Israel wander in the wilderness for forty years.

✳

The book of Deuteronomy tells us that those who broke the law could be punished by no more than forty lashes.

✳

After his baptism, Jesus spends forty days and forty nights in the wilderness, where he is tempted by the devil.

The Sacrifice of Noah. 1509-1512. Michelangelo Buonarroti. Sistine Chapel, Vatican.

And it came to pass at the end of forty days that Noah opened the window of the ark.

And he sent forth a dove to see if the waters were dried up. But the dove found no rest for her foot on the face of the whole earth, so she returned to him. He put forth his hand, and took her up into the ark. And he stayed yet another seven days, and again he sent forth the dove.

And in the evening she came to him, and lo, in her beak was an olive leaf plucked off. So Noah knew that the waters were abated from the earth.

He opened the ark, and behold, the face of the ground was dry. The ark rested upon the mountains of Ararat. And God spoke unto Noah, saying, "Go forth upon the earth. Bring with thee every living thing out of the ark."

So Noah went forth, and all the creatures with him, and builded an altar unto the Lord.

And God blessed Noah and his sons and said to them, "Be ye fruitful and replenish the earth. And, behold, I establish My covenant with you, and with your seed after you. Never will I again smite everything living, as I have done, neither shall there anymore be a flood to destroy the earth.

"And for My token of the covenant, which I make between Me and thee and all upon the earth after thee for every generation." I do set my bow in the cloud; and it shall come to pass when I bring a storm over the earth that the rainbow shall be seen in the cloud, and I will look on it and I will remember. The waters shall no more become a flood."

And out of the ark was the whole earth overspread. And the Lord smelled a sweet savor; and said in His heart, "I will not again curse the ground for man's sake. While the earth remaineth, seed time and harvest, and cold and heat, and summer and winter, and day and night, shall not cease."

OVERLEAF: *Noah's Sacrifice (detail)*. 1803. Joseph Anton Koch. Städelsches Kunstinstitut, Frankfurt.

"But Noah found grace in the eyes of the Lord."

What a wonderful line this is. When God observes that the world is corrupt, and that the hearts of men are filled with evil intent, we grieve with Him. But when Noah steps forth we can see a ray of hope. God is disappointed in His creation, but he will not abandon it. He will try once more to make a world that reflects His goodness.

This is a recurring theme in both the Old and New Testament. Again and again we are presented with evidence of human sin. But God always finds the righteous among the corrupt—men who can bear the burden and mark a new path for the rest of mankind. Men with whom God can enter into a new covenant.

Why does God single out Noah? We are told that "Noah was a just man in his generation" and that he "walked with God." But we are given no explanation of what is meant by this. Apparently, the author of the story felt that no further details were required. God saw something in Noah that pleased Him.

And when divine blessings are bestowed, the story seems to suggest, it is not for us to seek further explanation.

As we shall see in the stories of Abraham, Moses and others, God repeatedly chose unlikely leaders—men who did not initially stand out as giants by human standards, but who nevertheless proved to be men of profound faith.

NATIONS
DESCENDED
FROM NOAH
(GENESIS 10)

Abraham Visited by the Angels (detail). Mid-18th century. Giovanni Battista Tiepolo.
Museo del Prado, Madrid.

chapter 3

The Patriarchs

The first eleven chapters of the book of *Genesis*—which include the stories of the Creation and the Flood—deal with mankind in general. The remaining chapters concern themselves with a single people, the Israelites, and with the great patriarchs of that culture. The first of these patriarchs is Abraham.

In the story of Abraham, we encounter two of the great themes in Biblical literature: man's need for faith, and God's expectation of sacrifice. These themes are intertwined, of course. For, as each of these stories makes clear, it is our faith that will allow us to endure our sacrifices.

When God promises ninety-nine-year-old Abraham that "Kings shall come out of" him, Abraham questions how it can be so. After all, his wife, Sarah, cannot have children. Nevertheless, he continues to take God at His word. Later, when Abraham is called upon to make the greatest sacrifice of all—the deliverance of his only begotten son to God—he does not hesitate. And for that he is rewarded.

Abraham's reward, of course, pales in comparison to the reward God has in mind for his descendants. Eventually, they will enter the Promised Land.

Abraham and Isaac

Now of the sons of Noah—Shem, Ham and Japeth—after the flood: unto them were sons born, in their lands, in their families, and by these were the nations divided. The Lord scattered them abroad over the face of all the earth, the generations of Noah. They journeyed far, and the Lord dwelt in their tents.

They took wives and begat nations: Of the seed of Shem was Terah, who begat Abram in the land of Ur.

And the Lord appeared unto Abram, and said, "Get thee from the country, and from thy kindred, and from thy father's house unto a land that I will show thee. Unto thy seed will I give this land."

And Abram took Sarah, his wife, and all their substance, and went forth. But there was a famine, and the land could not bear them.

An expanse of wilderness near Egypt. Abraham is said to have journeyed throughout this region in accordance with God's command.

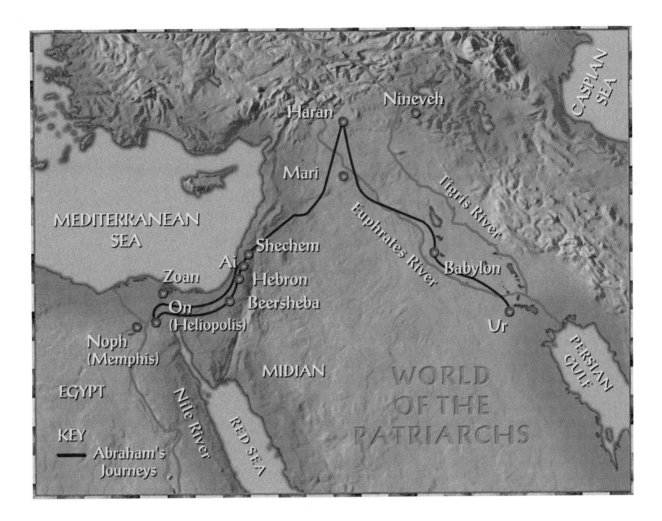

So Abram journeyed on, through Egypt, in the south, and returned at last to Canaan. And the Lord said unto Abram, "Lift up now thine eyes, and look. For all the land which thou seest, to thee I will give it, and to thy seed forever. Arise, walk through the land, and see."

Then Abram beheld all the plain of Hebron, well-watered as the garden of the Lord. And he dwelt there, and built an altar, saying "I lift up my hand unto the Lord, the possessor of Heaven and Earth."

Now Abram's wife bore him no children, and they waxed old, but believed in the Lord. And when Abram was ninety and nine, the Lord came to him in a vision and said to him, "I am the Lord that brought thee out of Ur to give thee this land. But know that thy seed shall be a stranger in a land that is not theirs."

The Ritual of Sacrifice

I will offer unto thee burnt sacrifices of fatlings, with the incense of rams...

PSALM 66

The practice of animal sacrifice was common among the early Israelites. Human sacrifice was another matter. Nevertheless, the belief that ritual sacrifices were important to God helps explain why Abraham complies with the divine order to make a "burnt offering" of his son.

Later books of the Bible offer different views of the subject of sacrifice. Some of the Psalms *reiterate the importance of the ritual, but others reflect a more sophisticated view. In* Psalm 51, *for example, we read: "For thou desirest not sacrifice; else would I give it: thou delightest not in burnt offering. The sacrifices of God are a broken spirit: a broken and contrite heart, O God, thou wilt not despise."*

In any event, according to the book of Hebrews, *the need for ritual sacrifices, animal or otherwise, came to an end when Christ obtained eternal redemption for us—not with "the blood of goats and calves, but by his own blood."*

And Abram fell on his face, but God talked with him saying, "Fear not, I am thy shield, the Almighty God. Walk thou before me, and be perfect. Thou shalt keep the way of the Lord, and I will know it."

Then the Lord said, "Neither shall thou be called Abram anymore: thy name shall be Abraham, for a father of many nations will I make thee."

And Abraham said, "Lord God, what wilt thou give me, seeing I go childless? Behold, thou has given me no seed."

The Lord said, "Kings shall come out of thee." And he brought him forth, saying, "Look now toward heaven, and count the stars, if thou be able to number them. So shall thy seed be."

And Abraham lifted his eyes, and looked, but Sarah laughed in her heart, thinking, "Shall a child be born to him that is old?"

And the Lord said, "Nay, but thou didst laugh. Is anything too hard for the Lord? Thou shall bear him a son. Ye shalt call his name Isaac. I will make him a great nation."

And the Lord went His way.

But God did as He had spoken, for Sarah conceived and bore a son unto Abraham.

And they called their son Isaac.

He held and kissed him, and said, "The smell of my son is as the smell of a field which the Lord hath planted." And he planted a grove and called there on the name of the Lord.

So the child grew.

But it came to pass that God did test Abraham. He came to his tent in the heat of the day and said to him, "Abraham, take now thy son, thine only son Isaac, whom thou lovest and get thee into the land of Moriah, and offer him there for a burnt offering."

So Abraham rose up early in the morning, and saddled his ass, and took two of his men with him,

and Isaac, his son, and the wood for the offering, and went as God told him.

And on the third day, Abraham lifted his eyes and saw the place afar off. And he said to his young men, "Wait ye here with the ass; I and the lad will go yonder and worship and come again to you."

And Abraham took the wood of the offering and laid it on Isaac, his son, to carry and he took in his hand, a knife; and they went, both of them together.

And Isaac spoke to Abraham, saying, "My father, here is the wood for the fire, but where is the lamb for the offering?"

And Abraham said, "My son, God will provide Himself a lamb." So they went together and came to

PREVIOUS PAGE: *Sacrifice of Isaac.* c. 1650. Rembrandt van Rijn. Hermitage, St. Petersburg.

RIGHT: *Mosque of the Dome of the Rock (interior), Jerusalem. The Mosque was built on the site where Abraham is said to have taken Isaac to be sacrificed.*

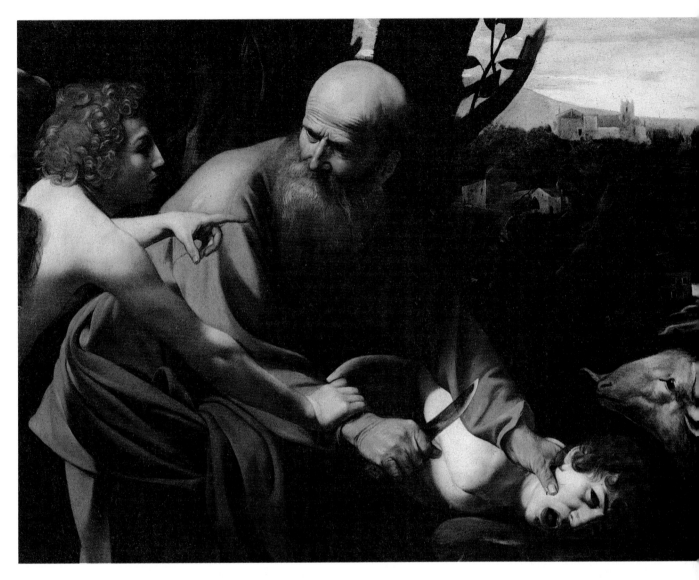

The Sacrifice of Isaac. c. 1591. Caravaggio. Galleria degli Uffizi, Florence.

the place which God had told him of. Abraham built an altar there, and laid the wood in order. Then he took Isaac, his son, and bound him and laid him upon the altar.

And Abraham stretched forth his hand, and took the knife to slay his son. But the angel of the Lord called him out of heaven, "Abraham, Abraham! Lay not thy hand upon the lad, saith the Lord, for now He knows that thou fearest God.

"And because thou hast not withheld thy son, thine only son, He will bless thee as the stars of heaven. And in thy seed shall all the nations of the earth be blessed;

because thou obeyed His voice."

So Abraham took up his son, and returned, saying, "Who can measure the spirit of the Lord? What man knows his plan?"

Joseph

Now among the sons of Isaac was Jacob, and his sons were twelve, but of them all, Jacob loved Joseph because he was the son of his old age. So he made him a coat of many colors.

And when his brethren saw that their father loved him more than all of them, they hated him.

And Joseph dreamed a dream, and he said to his brethren, "Hear this, I pray you: I dreamed we were binding sheaves in the field, and lo, my sheaf arose and stood upright; and your sheaves bowed down to mine."

And his brothers said to him, "Shalt thou indeed reign over us?" And they hated him yet the more.

So then, in envy, they conspired against him, saying "Behold this dreamer. Come let us slay him. We shall see what will become of his dreams."

But one of them, Judah, said, "Slay Joseph? Let not our hand be upon him; he is our brother; shed not his blood. Let us sell him into Egypt."

And so, when Joseph was among his brothers they stripped him of his coat, his coat of many colors, and they took him and sold him to some merchants for twenty pieces of silver, to be carried down into Egypt.

Then they killed a goat, and took Joseph's coat and dipped it in the blood. They took the coat to their father and said, "We found this; we know not if it is Joseph's."

But Jacob knew. He said, "It is my son's coat. Surely an evil beast hath devoured him."

His sons could not comfort him. He said, "I will go down to the grave mourning my son." And he wept for him.

Joseph Being Sold into Slavery. Anonymous.

The Twelve Tribes of Israel

According to the Bible, each of Jacob's twelve sons was an ancestor of one of the original tribes of Israel. The sons were born to four different mothers: Leah, Rachel and their respective maids, Bilhah and Zilpah.

Sons born to Leah: Reuben, Simeon, Levi, Judah, Issachar, Zebulun.

Sons born to Rachel: Joseph and Benjamin.

Sons born to Bilhah: Dan and Naphtali.

Son born to Zilpah: Gad and Asher.

While scholars are uncertain as to how this story relates to historical events, the idea of the twelve tribes endured into the time of Jesus and beyond. Indeed, it is no accident that Jesus recruited twelve disciples: "You who have followed Me," He tells them, "will also sit on twelve thrones, judging the twelve tribes of Israel." (Matthew 19:28)

So Joseph was brought down to Egypt. And Potiphar, the captain of Pharaoh's guard, bought him of those merchants who had taken him.

But the Lord was with Joseph. The Egyptian captain was a good man. Joseph found grace in his sight and served him well. So his master made him overseer of his house and all that he had.

And from that time the Lord blessed the Egyptian's house for Joseph's sake.

Now Joseph was a goodly and well-favored man. So it was that his master's wife cast her eyes upon him. And she said, "Lie with me."

But he said to her, "Behold, my master has committed all that he hath to my hand. He has kept back nothing from me, but thee, because thou art his wife! How then can I do this great wickedness, and sin against God?"

Still, she spoke to Joseph, day by day, to lie by her, to be with her. So one day Joseph went into the house, about his business, when none of the men of the house were there within.

And she caught his garment, saying, "Lie with me!" And he fled and left his garment in her hand.

When her lord came home and saw her, she said, "You have brought this Hebrew to mock us! He came to lie with me, and I cried out. He left his garment with me and fled."

So the master's wrath was kindled. He put Joseph into Pharaoh's prison.

Still, the Lord was with him.

The keeper of the prison committed to Joseph's hand all the prisoners: he had charge of them. And the Lord made all that he did to prosper.

Then it came to pass that the Pharaoh of Egypt was wroth against his chief steward and he put him into the prison where Joseph was held. And the captain of the guard charged Joseph to guard him well.

Jacob Receiving the Tunic of Joseph (detail). c. 1630. Diego Velázquez. Essorial, Madrid.

So when Joseph came to him in the morning and saw that he was sad, he asked, "Wherefore look ye sadly?"

And the steward answered, "I have dreamed a dream, and none can tell me its meaning."

And Joseph said, "Meanings belong to God. Tell me your dream."

And the steward said, "In my dream were three branches of ripe grapes. I took the grapes and pressed them into Pharaoh's cup, and put the cup in his hand."

And Joseph said, "This is the meaning. The three branches are three days: within three days shall Pharaoh restore thee to thy place, his steward, as before. But think on me when all shall be well with thee, I pray

*Joseph and the Wife of Potiphar
(detail).* c. 1550-1555. Jacopo
Tintoretto. Museo del Prado,
Madrid.

thee. For indeed I was stolen away out of the land of
the Hebrews, and here they have put me into this dungeon, though I have done nothing."

And on the third day, it came to pass as Joseph had
foretold: Pharaoh freed his steward from the prison and
restored him again to his place. Yet the man forgot
Joseph in his dungeon.

But there came a time when Pharaoh had a dream of
seven cattle coming up out of the river, fat and well-
favored, and they fed in a meadow. Then out of the
river behind them came seven other cattle, lean and ill-

favored, and they did eat up the seven fat cattle.

So Pharaoh awoke, sore-troubled. He sent for all the magicians of Egypt, and the wise men as well, and told them his dream. But none could tell its meaning.

Then said his chief steward, "I do remember when my lord put me in prison, I dreamed a dream. And a young Hebrew there told me the meaning, and it came to pass as he told me: I am restored to my office."

So Pharaoh sent for Joseph, and they brought him hastily out of the dungeon. And Pharaoh said, "I have dreamed a dream, and none can interpret it. I have heard said of thee that thou understand dreams."

And Joseph answered Pharaoh, "It is not in me: God

Joseph Explaining the Dreams of Pharaoh. Jean Adrien-Guignet. Musée des Beaux-Arts, Rouen.

shall give Pharaoh an answer."

So Pharaoh told Joseph his dream, and Joseph said, "What God is about to do, He shows thee. Behold, there come seven years of plenty throughout all of Egypt. But then shall come seven years of famine. The years of plenty shall be forgotten; famine shall consume the land of Egypt.

"Now therefore let Pharaoh find a man discreet and wise. In the seven plenteous years, let him gather all the food of those good years, and hold it in store against the seven years of famine, which shall surely come. So Egypt will not perish."

And Pharaoh said to Joseph, "Since God hath showed thee all of this, there is none so discreet and wise as thou. A man in whom is the spirit of God.

"By thy word shall my people be ruled. I will set thee over all the land. Only I will be greater than thou."

Then Pharaoh took off his ring and put it on Joseph's hand, and arrayed him in fine linen, with a gold chain about his neck. He said, "I am Pharaoh, but without thee shall no man lift up his hand in all of Egypt."

And it was so. Joseph went throughout the land as the hand of Pharaoh. He said, "God hath caused me to be fruitful in the land of my affliction."

And in the seven plenteous years the earth was bountiful. But Joseph laid up a fifth part of the food of those years and stored it against the lean years to come.

So when the famine came over all the earth, Joseph opened all the store-houses, and there was bread in Egypt, while the famine waxed sore.

Now all the countries came into Egypt to buy corn; because the famine was in their lands.

And the brothers of Joseph came too, and stood before him. But they knew him not.

So Joseph said to them, "Come closer, I pray you." And when they came near, he said, "I am Joseph, your brother, whom ye sold into Egypt. Does my father yet live?"

And they fell down before him, but he said, "Fear

not. Am I in the place of God? Be not grieved that ye sold me into Egypt to deliver you. It was not you that put me here but God. Ye thought evil against me, but God meant it to bring good. He hath made me a lord in the house of the Pharaoh and through all Egypt.

"So now haste ye, my brothers! To my father, and bring him hither. Ye shall dwell in Egypt, and here will I nourish thee."

And they went up out of Egypt, back again to Jacob their father and told him, "Joseph is yet alive. He is lord over all Egypt." And Jacob's heart trembled; he believed them not. But when he saw the wagons Joseph had sent to carry him, his spirit rose. He said, "My son is yet alive. I will go see him before I die."

And Jacob journeyed with all that he had, and while he slept by the way, God came to him in the visions of the night, saying, "Jacob, Jacob, fear not to go down into Egypt; for there I will make of thee a great nation.

"Thy name shall be called Jacob no more, but Israel." So, blessed by God, Jacob and all his seed, his sons and his sons' sons came into Egypt.

When Joseph saw his father, they embraced and wept for a long time. At last Joseph said, "The Lord watched between me and thee when we were absent one from another."

Israel said only, "Now let me die, since I have seen thy face."

"My brethren and my father's house are come unto me," said Joseph.

And Pharaoh said, "All Egypt is before thee; in the best of the land shall ye dwell."

So the children of Israel dwelt in Egypt, and multiplied. And these were the twelve tribes of Israel.

And Joseph, he was a fruitful bough. His hands were made strong by the mighty God of his fathers; the shepherd, the stone of Israel.

OVERLEAF: *Joseph Recognized by His Brethren.* Baron Françoise Pascal Gerard.

The Great Pyramids of Giza. In some Biblical stories, Egypt is a safe haven. After Jesus is born, for example, Mary and Joseph take him to Egypt so that he will not be killed. In other stories, such as those told in the next chapter, it represents foreign oppression.

In the final chapter of the book of *Genesis*, Joseph dies. But the story ends on a note of hope. On his death bed, he tells his brothers that "God will surely come to you and bring you up out of this land to the land he swore to Abraham and Isaac, and to Jacob."

Having been rescued from famine by Joseph, his brothers have no reason to question his prophecy. But subsequent generations will have their faith shaken many times before God's promise is fulfilled.

Why does God wait so long to lead His chosen people into the Promised Land? The great patriarchs must have asked themselves that question countless times. They are, after all, only human. Men of deep faith and humility—but men nonetheless. God, apparently, does not wish them to fully understand His purposes.

In time, of course, He will fulfill His promise, even though the Israelites and their leaders sometimes act in ways that are contrary to His plans. As Shakespeare put it in Hamlet: "There's a divinity that shapes our ends, rough-hew them how we will."

Israel in Egypt (detail). 1867. Sir Edward Poynter. Guildhall Art Gallery, London.

chapter 4

Bondage in Egypt

The good will that Joseph had earned for his people in Egypt was not destined to endure. In the very first chapter of the book of *Exodus,* we learn of a new Egyptian king "who did not know Joseph." Alarmed by the increasing numbers of Israelites—who are known to worship one God—the king forces them into slavery. And so, another period of hardship begins.

Now God must choose a new leader to act on His behalf. He chooses Moses—a man who begins life as an outcast and later becomes a fugitive; a simple man who has a reputation as being "slow of speech." Once again, it is a curious choice. Indeed, when God calls upon him, even Moses himself protests that he is unworthy.

"Who am I," he asks, "that I should go to bring Israel out of bondage?"

But in asking this question, Moses is revealing his humility—a quality he shares with the other heroes of the Old Testament. Ultimately, this humility will lead him to the realization that he, personally, can never bring Israel out of bondage. That is God's role. Nevertheless, as God's agent, he must *act* in accordance with God's plan. To do so, he must learn to have faith in himself as well as in God.

And the children of Israel were fruitful; the land was filled with them.

But at last there arose a new king over Egypt, and he said, "The children of Israel are more and mightier than we. Come, let us deal wisely, lest they multiply and join against us."

Therefore he set taskmasters over them; they made the children of Israel serve bitterly in hard bondage in the field, making brick; but still they multiplied.

So Pharaoh charged all his people, saying, "These Hebrews shall find no ease; never shall the soles of their feet have rest. In the morning they shall say, 'Would God it were night!' and in the night they shall say, 'Would God it were morning!'

"The sword without, and terror within, shall destroy them, and the heart of Israel shall be cast down. Now therefore destroy every male among their little ones; every son that is born, ye shall cast into the river, that I

BELOW: *Scenes from the Life of Moses (detail).* Botticelli. Sistine Chapel, Vatican.

may lift up my hand to heaven and say, 'I live forever.'"

But now the spirit of God moved in the land; Jochabel, wife of Amram, conceived and bore a son. He was a goodly child; when she saw him, she said, "He shall live!" And she hid him three months.

And when she could no longer hide him, she made for him a basket of bulrushes, and daubed it with pitch, and put the child there inside, and she laid it in the reeds by the river's edge.

And his sister hid nearby to see what would be done to him.

Now the daughter of Pharaoh came down to bathe in the river, with her maidens. She walked by the water, and when she saw the basket among the reeds, she sent her maids to fetch it.

When she opened it, she saw the child; and, behold,

ABOVE: *Moses Saved from the Waters.* 1638. Nicolas Poussin. The Louvre, Paris.

OVERLEAF: *Israel in Egypt (full view).*

The Pharaoh of Exodus

Many Biblical scholars believe that the enslavement of the Israelites in Egypt was initiated by Rameses the Second, who ruled from 1279 to 1212 B.C. The pyramids were already a thousand years old when Rameses was born, but he built lesser monuments all over Egypt and Nubia.

While Rameses the Second may also have been in power during the Exodus itself, some scholars believe that this event took place during the reign of his son, Merenptah. A record of Merenptah's military victories contains the words, "Israel is desolated and has no seed."

According to James Weinstein of Cornell University, this is the first documented mention of Israel in the ancient Near East.

the babe wept; and she took pity on him and said, "This is one of the Hebrews' children."

She said, "I will take this child; he shall be my son, and a prince over all men. And because I drew him out of the water, his name shall be called Moses!"

And so, at last, it came to pass that when Moses was grown he went out of the city to his brethren; and when he saw an Egyptian striking one of the Hebrews, Moses' anger waxed hot; he lifted his hand and slew the Egyptian.

Then Moses said, "Surely, when this thing is known, Pharaoh will slay me!" So he fled from the wrath of Egypt, and came at last to the land of Midian, and dwelt there, and kept the flocks of Jethro.

And Jethro gave Moses his daughter Ziphorah; and she bore him a son, and Moses was content. He said, "I have been a stranger in a strange land."

But in Egypt, the children of Israel cried in their bondage, and their cry came up to God.

And God heard them, and remembered.

The Burning Bush

Now in the desert of Midian, where Moses kept his flocks, he came to the mountain of God, called Sinai. And he looked and beheld a bush that burned with fire; but the bush was not consumed.

And Moses said, "I will turn aside to see this great sight." And when he had climbed to this place, God called to him out of the midst of the fire, "Moses! Moses!" and he said, "I am here!"

And the Voice said, "Put off thy shoes from off thy

OPPOSITE: *The Finding of Moses.* 16th century. Raphael.

BELOW: *The Finding of Moses by Pharaoh's Daughter.* 1904. Sir Lawrence Alma-Tadema. Private Collection.

OVERLEAF: *Scenes from the Life of Moses.* Botticelli. Sistine Chapel, Vatican.

The Monastery of St. Catherine—the world's oldest surviving

Christian monastery—near the foot of Mount Sinai. Within the

monastery is the Shrine of the Burning Bush. It is believed that Moses

was in this vicinity when he first heard the voice of God.

feet, for the place whereon thou standest is holy ground.

"I am the God of thy fathers, the God of Abraham, the God of Isaac, and the God of Jacob."

And Moses hid his face; he was afraid to look upon God.

And the Lord said, "I have surely seen the affliction of My people which are in Egypt and heard their cries, for I know their sorrows. Therefore will I send thee, Moses, and thou shalt bring forth My people to serve Me upon this mountain."

And Moses said, "Who am I, Lord, that I should go to bring Israel out of bondage?

"Behold, when I come to the people and say to them, 'The God of your fathers has sent me,' they will not believe me. They shall say, 'What is His name?' And how shall I answer them?"

And God said to Moses, "I AM THAT I AM! Thou shalt say I AM hath sent Me to you!

"This is My name forever; and they will believe thee. Now therefore, go; and I will be with thee!"

OVERLEAF: *Moses Before the Burning Bush.* c. 1516. Raphael's workshop. Loggia, Vatican.

The more you read the Bible, the more you discover parallels between the Old and New Testaments. The similarities between the stories of Moses and Jesus are especially interesting. Both were men of humble parents, and as adults they never rose above their modest social status. (Moses, remember, was a shepherd, while Jesus was a carpenter.) Both performed miracles as a way of convincing people that they spoke on behalf of God. But before either of them can go about God's business, they must endure self-imposed exile in the desert, or wilderness.

Their experiences in the wilderness are different, of course. For Jesus, the central experience is temptation: Satan tests him, and he responds with divine insight. For Moses, the encounter with the burning bush is a moment of instruction. He is a good man, presumably, but lacks divine wisdom.

Indeed, neither Jews, nor Christians, nor Muslims regard Moses as divine. He is, in all three religious traditions, a man who is as flawed as the rest of us. But he is a great man nevertheless—Lawgiver and Deliverer to the Jews, warrior prophet to Muslims, first among prophets to Christians.

To Christ, he was especially important. "If ye believe Moses," Jesus is reported to have said, "so shall ye believe me."

Moses Before the Burning Bush. c. 1614. Domenico Fetti. Kunsthistoriches Museum, Vienna.

The Delivery of Israel Out of Egypt. 19th or early 20th century. Samuel Coleman.

chapter 5

Let My People Go

The story of Moses' confrontation with the Pharaoh is among the most dramatic of all the tales in the Bible. Again, we see how God's wrath is felt by sinners—in this case, the Egyptians who are guilty of oppressing the Israelites.

When Moses initially approaches the Pharaoh, he simply reports God's declaration: "Let my people go!" Not surprisingly, the Pharaoh—who considers himself to be god-like—refuses to recognize the authority of which Moses speaks. Instead, he tightens his grip on the Israelites, making life even more difficult than it had been. The people complain to Moses, in a foreshadowing of what Moses will have to put up with in the wilderness, after their escape from Egypt.

But with God at his side, Moses is persistent. If the Pharaoh will not relent, God, acting through Moses, will make him suffer. He orders Moses to initiate a series of ten horrible plagues, beginning with the turning of the waters of the Nile into blood and ending with the slaughter of all the first-born in Egypt.

Plagues as Punishment for Sin

There are several instances in the Old Testament of God using plagues as a means of punishment. In Genesis, the Lord brings "great plagues" upon Pharaoh and his house because the Pharaoh has tried to take Abram's wife, Sarai, (later renamed Abraham and Sarah) as his own.

On occasion, God also warns the Israelites that He will send plagues upon them if they break divine law. (See Leviticus, 26:25 and Exodus, 32:35)

Many scholars believe that the concept of plagues was rooted in natural phenomena common to Egypt and the Holy Land in ancient times. It is likely, for example, that infestations of frogs and insects were common to the region.

Other plagues mentioned in the Bible, such as the turning of the Nile into blood, are more mysterious. Some scholars have suggested that the Nile may have occassionally taken on a blood-like appearance when red clay was washed down from the river's source.

So Moses went, and returned into Egypt, with his wife and his sons, and the staff of God in his hand.

And, with his brother, Aaron, he went in to Pharaoh and told him, "Thus saith the Lord God of Israel, 'Let my people go!'"

And Pharaoh said, "Who is this God that I should obey his voice? I know not thy God, neither will I let Israel go. You will keep these people from their labor with your vain words.

The Moses Fountain. Claus Sluter. Chartreuse de Champnol, Dijon.

"They are idle, idle, and you make them rest.

"Therefore there shall be more work for them. Go, tell them, 'Thus saith Pharaoh, "I shall not give you straw to make brick, as before!"' Let them gather straw for themselves. But the tally of bricks must not lessen! Go now, and work."

And when Moses and Aaron came forth from Pharaoh, the people turned from them, saying, "Wherefore did you so? You put a sword in their hands to slay us."

And Moses said in his heart, "Lord, why hast Thou sent me in Thy name?"

But the Lord said to Moses, "I will make thee as a god to Pharaoh. Go again to him.

"Take thy staff and stretch forth thy hand upon the river. You shall multiply the wonders in the land, and in this shall they know that I am the Lord."

ABOVE: *The Seventh Plague of Egypt.* 19th century. J.M.W. Turner. Indianapolis Museum of Art.

OVERLEAF: *Departure of the Israelites.* David Roberts. Birmingham City Art Museum, Birmingham.

And Moses did as the Lord commanded. He lifted up his staff in the sight of the Pharaoh and struck the waters; and all the river turned to blood. Throughout the land of Egypt, the waters turned to blood. And the fish died and the river stank, and the Egyptians could not drink.

But the heart of Pharaoh hardened; he harkened not.

So Moses said to him, "That thou mayest know there is none like unto the Lord." And he smote the dust of the earth with his staff, and the dust became lice.

Pharaoh's magicians could do nothing; there were lice upon man and beast. And the frogs came up out of the river, and covered up the land, and they died in the houses in heaps.

Then came swarms of flies; the land stank and the cattle died. The people were stricken with sores, save only the children of Israel.

And the ministers of Pharaoh said, "This is the finger of God." But Pharaoh would not listen. He drove Moses and Aaron from his presence.

Then did Moses stretch forth his hand to heaven, and the Lord rained hail upon the earth, fire ran along the ground, and there was a thick darkness over all the land for three days. The earth was covered and the green things broken.

And Pharaoh's ministers cried to him, "How long shall this man be on us? Let them go, that they may serve their God. Knowest thou not yet that Egypt is destroyed?"

Then Pharaoh called for Moses, and said, "Take away from me this death!"

And Moses spread his hands, and the thunders ceased, and he said, "How long wilt thou refuse to humble thyself? Thus saith the Lord of Israel, 'Let My people go!'"

And Pharaoh said, "Get thee from me!'"

So Moses said, "Yet the Lord will bring one more plague upon Egypt. About midnight, will the Lord smite your firstborn, from Pharaoh on his throne to the captives in his dungeons. And against the children of Israel shall not a dog move his tongue."

And Pharaoh said in anger, "Take heed you see my face no more, for on the day you see my face again you shall surely die."

And Moses said, "Thou hast spoken well. I will see thy face no more." And he turned and went out from the city.

Then Moses called for all the elders of Israel, and said to them, "This day shall be the beginning to you, for the Lord hath spoken. Make ready to eat in haste this night, of unleavened bread and lamb. And let each man take the blood of the lamb and mark the door of his house; and none shall go out till the morning.

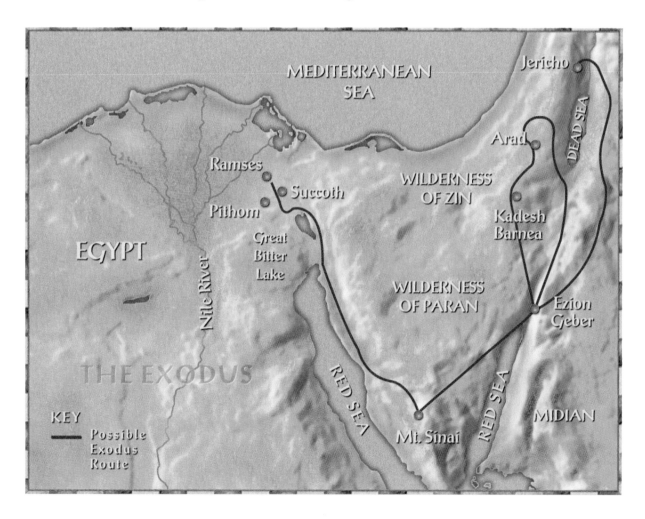

The Crossing of the Red Sea

The precise route of the Exodus has not been determined. Some scholars believe that the Israelites passed to the north of the Red Sea, in the region of the Bitter Lakes (see map). Other historians have suggested that they crossed the northern tip of the Red Sea's western "finger," which today is known as the Gulf of Suez.

In any case, the story of the parting of the waters remains a mystery. Scientists have theorized that a steady wind, blowing over a period of several hours, could have lowered the water level enough to allow the Israelites to pass on foot. When the winds died down, so the theory goes, the waters came rushing back to their normal level.

Whatever the case may be, the story of Moses parting the Red Sea remains captivating.

Like the story of the Flood, it gives us a sense of God's awesome power—and reinforces the idea that justice will triumph.

"For tonight will the Lord smite the Egyptians. When He sees the mark upon your doors, He will not suffer the destroyer to come in, but pass over your house. And this day shall ye remember forever."

And the people bowed their heads and did as the Lord commanded.

And at midnight it came to pass, as Moses said, all the firstborn of Egypt were struck; there was not a house where there was not one dead, and a great cry rose up, "We be all dead men!"

And Pharaoh rose up in the night and called from his throne, "Get ye forth from among my people. Go! Serve your God and be gone."

The Crossing of the Red Sea

And Moses said, "We will go, with our young and with our old, with our sons and with our daughters; with our flocks and with our herds will we go. We have seen this day that God liveth!"

And the children of Israel did go, up out of Egypt, in a mixed multitude, on foot with their flocks and herds.

And Moses said to the people, "Hear, O Israel! Remember this day, when the strong hand of the Lord brings you out of bondage."

And the Lord went before them as a pillar of cloud to lead the way, and by night a pillar of fire. So they came at last through the desert to the Red Sea and camped there.

But then the Pharaoh was told where they fled, and his heart was turned again. He said, "Why have we done this, to let Israel go?" So he took his chariot, and all the chariots in Egypt, with captains over every one, and pursued the children of Israel, encamping by the sea.

Now when they beheld Pharaoh's host drawing near, they were sore afraid, and cried out to Moses, "Were

there no graves in Egypt? Hast thou taken us away to die in the wilderness?"

But Moses said, "Hold your peace. The Lord shall fight for you."

Moses stretched out his hand, over the sea, and the waters were divided, and made the sea dry land. And the children of Israel went in the midst, and the waters were a wall on the right and on the left.

But the Egyptians pursued—all Pharaoh's host—after them through the sea.

Then Moses said, "Fear not. Stand still, and see the salvation of the Lord." Again he stretched forth his hand, and the waters returned over all the host; not one remained.

The Children of Israel in the Wilderness. c. 1519. Fresco School of Raphael. Loggia, Vatican.

And Moses cried, "Who is like unto Thee O Lord? Thou didst blow with Thy wind, and the sea covered them. Who shall live when Thou doest this? Thou hast borne us out of Egypt, as an eagle bears his young upon his wings."

One of the many monuments built by Ramses II.

The victory of the Israelites over the Pharaoh and his powerful Egyptian army has inspired countless artists. The story is compelling in large part because it is such a powerful expression of hope and faith. But equally fascinating is the story of the Pharaoh's fall. Here, after all, is a man who initially appears to be all-powerful but is, in the end, brought down by his own wickedness.

The irony of this story is summed up beautifully in "Ozymandias," a poem by the great Romantic poet Percy Bysshe Shelley. In the poem, Shelley writes of a crumbling monument to the once great Pharaoh Rameses, whose throne name was Usermatre. (Over the centuries, this became Ozymandias.)

The engraving on the monument's pedestal is still clear: "My name is Ozymandias, king of kings: Look on my works, ye Mighty, and despair!" But the works are mighty no more. Instead, the visage of the Egyptian leader lies "shattered" and "half sunk" in the sand. And "Round the decay of that colossal wreck, boundless and bare, The lone and level sands stretch far away."

The poem is reminiscent of God's warning to Adam after the Fall: "For dust you are," He says, "and to dust you shall return." It also brings to mind Jesus' admonition against accumulating "treasures of the earth, where moth and rust consume . . ." Jesus urges his followers to concentrate instead on storing up "treasures in heaven . . . . For where your treasure is, there your heart will be also."

Like Jesus, Moses is aware of this fundamental truth. For that reason, he is, from the beginning, unimpressed with the Pharaoh's riches. He adheres to the belief that only God—and God's works—will endure forever. That belief gives him the courage to stand up to the Pharaoh. And it gives him the strength to withstand the many difficulties that lie ahead as he leads his people toward the Promised Land.

The Red Sea.

Moses Presenting the Stone Tablets. Raphael. Stanza di Eliodoro, Vatican.

chapter 6

Toward the Promised Land

Through the final four Books of Moses—*Exodus, Leviticus, Numbers* and *Deuteronomy*—God gives him very specific and detailed instructions on many matters: specifications for the construction of the Ark of the Covenant, rules of worship and sacrifice, and all sorts of laws governing social conduct. Apparently, Moses commits them all to memory. Indeed, throughout both Testaments of the Bible, God only writes down His instructions once— when He delivers the Ten Commandments.

Initially God delivers the Commandments orally—"with a great voice." But immediately thereafter, He gives Moses two stone tablets "written with the finger of God." The phrase, "written in stone," has since become a common expression of permanence. You're not likely to change something carved in stone, especially if it has been written in God's hand. Perhaps that's why the Ten Commandments have endured and have become the cornerstone of ethical philosophy of Western civilization.

So Moses brought Israel through the wilderness. They went many days and found no water. And the people were sore afraid.

But Moses said to them, "Ye murmur in your tents, yet you have seen how the Lord sustains you as a man doth carry his son, in all the ways that ye go. He knoweth thy walking through this great wilderness, you have lacked nothing. The Lord brings you unto a good land, a land of brooks of water, of fountains and depths that spring out of valleys and hills.

Moses Strikes the Rock. James Jacques Joseph Tissot. Jewish Museum, New York.

Moses Causes Water to Gush from the Rock. Raphael. Loggia, Vatican.

"That land drinketh of the rain of heaven! He will give you water in due season; the first rain and the last.

"He humbles you and suffers you to thirst, that He might make you know that man does not live by bread only.

"The Lord did not choose you because ye were more in number than any people, for ye were the fewest. But because the Lord loved you. He redeemed you from the hand of Pharaoh.

"He leads you through a wilderness of scorpions and drought, where there is no water, who can bring forth water out of flint. So beware, lest you forget Him, who brought you forth out of Egypt."

But still the people went all that night, crying, "What shall we drink? Would God we had died in Egypt. Wherefore has the Lord brought us into this land; to perish here? Let us make a captain and return to Egypt."

And Moses said, "Hear now, ye rebels; must we fetch you water out of the rock?" And he lifted his hand, and with his staff struck the rock twice; and water came out, sweet and abundant, and the people drank, and camped there, by the waters.

The Gathering of Manna in the Desert.
1660-1664. Nicolas Poussin.
The Louvre, Paris.

Then the Lord spoke to Moses, saying, "I have heard the murmurings of Israel. I will rain food from the heavens for you. Speak to them and say so." And in the morning it was so; on the ground lay food like the frost.

And Moses said, "This is the bread the Lord hath given you; it is manna. Take it and eat."

And they did so; they took of the food of the Lord in their hands and the taste of it was like honey.

So the multitude went on, the many thousands of Israel, journeying to the land which the Lord had promised; through days of gladness and solemn days, and the glory of the Lord was on them, through all their journeys.

But at last the people wept again, and chided Moses, saying, "Who shall give us meat to eat? We did eat in Egypt freely: fish, cucumbers, and the melons; but now there is nothing but this manna."

And Moses heard them, and said to the Lord, "What shall I do with these people? They be almost ready to stone me.

"Have I conceived them? Did I father them that Thou should say to me, 'Carry them in thy bosom'?

"They wept to me, saying, 'Give us meat.' Where should I have meat for all these people?

"Shall the flocks and the herds be slain for them, or all the fish of the sea? I am not able to bear all this; it is too heavy for me."

And the Lord said unto Moses, "Is the Lord's hand waxed short? Thou shalt see now whether My word shall come to pass or not."

And Moses went out and told the people, "The Lord will give you meat, and ye shall eat; not one day, nor ten days, but a month, until it comes out your nostrils. Because we wept before Him, 'Why came we out of Egypt?'"

But Miriam and Aaron spoke against Moses. They said, "Hath the Lord indeed spoken only through Moses?"

A campsite in the Sinai desert, the "wilderness" in which the Israelites wandered for forty years under the leadership of Moses.

And there was a young man named Joshua. And Joshua said, "My Lord Moses, forbid them!"

But Moses said, "Dost thou envy me? Would God that all the people were prophets, so the Lord would put his spirit upon them!" And Moses and the elders went into the camp.

But there came forth a wind now, and the Lord spoke suddenly to Moses and Aaron and Miriam. "Hear now My words; if there were a prophet among you, I would make Myself known to him. My servant is Moses; with him will I speak."

Then Moses said to them, "Now ye have heard the voice of God. I stand between the Lord and you, lest ye be afraid. God is not a man, that He should lie. Hath He spoken, and shall He not make it good?

"Because he loved your fathers, He brought you out of Egypt. Therefore rise up, Israel!

"We have stayed long enough in this place; turn you and take your journey into the great river.

"Strong is thy dwelling place; ye have set thy nest in a rock. Only take heed, lest ye forget your God."

Receiving the Tablets of the Law

Then, after three months, they came at last to the Wilderness of Sinai, and camped there before the mountain. And it came to pass in the morning that there were thunders and a thick cloud upon the mount. Then came a voice of a trumpet, and the people trembled, and the mountain quaked.

But Moses said, "Fear not. God is come; to prove you." And he climbed up into the thick darkness where God was. He stayed many days and many nights, cloud covering the glory of the Lord.

But when he came not down, the people gathered

OVERLEAF: *Moses Receiving the Tablets of Law.* c. 1514. Raphael. Stanza di Eliodoro, Vatican.

Adoration of the Golden Calf (detail). Jacopo Tintoretto. S. Maria dell'Orto, Venice.

before Aaron and said to him, "Up Aaron! You shall make us gods to go before us. As for this Moses, we know not what is become of him."

So Aaron said to them, "Break off the golden rings from the ears of your wives and your daughters, and bring them to me." And the people did so; they stripped off their ornaments, all the spoils of Egypt, and brought them to Aaron. And he beat the gold into plates, and fashioned a golden calf, and said, "This be thy God, O Israel!"

Yet afar off on the mount, Moses drew near where God was, and heard him, "Now hearken, Moses. I teach you, that they may live. I declare unto you My ten commandments. Let them not depart from thy heart all the days of thy life, but teach them."

Then these words the Lord spoke, with a great voice:

I AM THE LORD THY GOD. THOU SHALT HAVE NO OTHER
    GODS BEFORE ME.

THOU SHALT NOT MAKE UNTO THEE ANY GRAVEN IMAGE.

THOU SHALT NOT TAKE THE NAME OF THE LORD THY GOD
    IN VAIN.

REMEMBER THE SABBATH DAY, TO KEEP IT HOLY.

HONOR THY FATHER AND THY MOTHER, THAT THY DAYS
    MAY BE LONG IN THE LAND.

THOU SHALT NOT KILL.

THOU SHALT NOT COMMIT ADULTERY.

THOU SHALT NOT STEAL.

THOU SHALT NOT BEAR FALSE WITNESS.

THOU SHALT NOT COVET ANYTHING THAT IS THY
    NEIGHBOR'S.

And the Lord spoke with Moses as a man speaks to his friend, and when He had made an end, He gave him two tablets of stone, written with the finger of God, and the writing was the word of God.

Versions of the Ten Commandments

The Ten Commandments, also known as the Decalogue, actually appear twice in the Bible: once in Exodus 20, *and again in* Deuteronomy 5.

In each instance, the list begins with the words, "I am the Lord your God who brought you out of the land of Egypt, out of the house of slavery." Christians generally regard this as a prologue. To the Jews, however, it is considered the first Commandment. Judaism combines the lines "Thou shalt have no other gods..." and the prohibition against graven images, or idols, into a single second Commandment.

Roman Catholics and Lutherans also combine these two lines and consider them to be part of the first Commandment. In these traditions, there are still ten Commandments, however, because the final law—which warns against coveting "thy neighbor's wife, his manservant, his maidservant, his ox, his donkey and anything else that is thy neighbors"—is divided in two.

The slopes of Mount Sinai, which is also called Jebel Musa, or

"Mountain of Moses." Yet another name for Mount Sinai

is Mount Horeb. While these names are frequently used

interchangeably, some scholars believe that Horeb actually

refers to a separate mountain in the same vicinity.

The Breaking of the Tablets

When Moses turned and went down from the Mount his face shone. So he came to where Joshua waited, and Joshua said, "There is a noise of war in the camp."

But Moses heard the voice of God, who said, "Go, get thee down! For thy people have corrupted themselves."

And they came to the camp where the people drank and played naked before the golden calf. And Moses saw this, and his anger waxed hot, and he cried out, "Hath the Lord brought you out of the iron furnace to be unto Him as ye are this day?"

And Moses cast the tablets from his hands, and broke them beneath the calf. And the people feared, and the wicked fell on their faces. But then the fire went out from the Lord; the earth opened and swallowed all. They went down alive into the pit, and the earth closed upon them. They died before the Lord.

Till, at last, Moses stood between the dead and the

Moses Destroying the Golden Calf.
1681. Andrea Celesti.
Palazzo Ducale, Venice.

living, saying, "Now pardon this people, I beseech Thee, in Thy mercy. Hold off Thy fierce wrath, O Lord! Or blot me from Thy book."

And the plague was stayed.

But the Lord's anger was kindled against Israel. He made them wander in the wilderness forty years, until all the generation that had done evil was consumed.

The Last Days of Moses

At last there came a morning on the plains of Moab, when the Lord said to Moses, "Rise up! Moses, RISE UP! Get thee up this mountain and behold the land which I give unto Israel.

"Thou shall see that land before thee. But thou may not go thither. Thou shall be gathered unto me, and I shall give thee rest."

And Moses said, "Let the congregation of the Lord

Moses with the Tablets of Law.
1630. Guido Reni.

be not as sheep which have no shepherd. Set before them a man who can lead them."

And the Lord said, "Take thee Joshua. Put some of thine honor upon him, and they shall put thy name upon the children."

So Moses turned towards the camp. He was old, but his eye was not dim. He said, "How goodly are thy tents, O Israel."

Then he called the elders to him, saying, "Hear, O Israel! Thou art to pass over Jordan this day. I have led you forty years in the wilderness, where ye groped at noonday, as the blind grope in darkness. Ye have been a rebellious people from the day I knew you; yet ye are my people.

"And behold, ye are this day as the stars of heaven, a multitude. May the Lord God make ye a thousand times many more than you are. May He bless you, and keep you, and none make you afraid."

Then Moses called Joshua. He laid his hands on him and said, "Be strong and of good courage; for thou must lead this people into the new land. The Lord was angry with me for your sakes. He said that I may not

THE PROMISED LAND

MEDITERRANEAN SEA

CANAAN

AMMON

SEA OF GALILEE

Jordan River

Ai · Jericho ·

DEAD SEA

KEY
· Town Conquered by Joshua

Lachish ·

· Hebron

Debir ·

MOAB

EDOM

OVERLEAF: The Dome of the Rock, Jerusalem.

go over Jordan. I must die in this land; but ye shall go over, all shall go, and possess that good land.

"And when the Lord shall have brought thee to that land He swore to thy fathers; a land of wheat and honey where ye shall lack nothing; with houses full of all good things, which ye build not; and vines and olive trees which ye plant not; when ye shall have eaten and are full, then keep thou these words in thy heart and let not the people forget what your eyes have seen.

"Love ye, therefore, the stranger; for ye were strangers in Egypt.

"When ye cut harvest in the field, and forget a sheaf, go not again to get it. Let it be for the stranger, for the fatherless and the widow.

"So you shall remember that ye were slaves in Egypt.

"Between your brethren and the stranger, judge righteously, for all men are brothers.

"Be not afraid; if ye turn aside from God, then the anger of the Lord shall smoke against you. But if ye seek the Lord, ye shall find Him, if ye seek with all your heart and soul.

"The Lord thy God is a merciful God; when ye are in tribulation, if ye turn to the Lord He will not foresake you.

"And as I truly live, all the earth shall be filled with the glory of the Lord.

"Now go, proclaim liberty throughout all the lands, unto all the inhabitants thereof."

Thus Moses blessed Israel, and they harkened unto him. Then Joshua led the host over Jordan. And Moses went up into the mountain of Nebo, and the Lord showed him all the Promised Land, from Gilea and Judea unto the utmost sea.

Then God said to him, "This is thy place." So Moses died there.

No man knows his sepulchre, unto this day.

But there arose not a prophet since in Israel like unto Moses, whom the Lord knew, face to face.

Of Judges and Kings . . .

After Joshua's death, according to the Bible, the Israelites began to worship Canaanite deities. When God punished them by allowing them to fall under the control of their enemies, they repented. In an effort to keep the people on the path of righteousness, God chose a series of leaders known as "judges." (The most famous of these leaders is Samson.)

Sometime after that—perhaps around 1000 B.C.—this system of judges was replaced by a monarchy. The first king was named Saul, but his reign was relatively brief. According to the book of Samuel, Saul fell from grace after refusing to obey a divine command.

The greatest of all kings was David, who managed to unite Israel and Judah into a single nation. This unification continued under the leadership of David's son, Solomon, but could not be maintained after Solomon's death, which is estimated to be around 924 B.C.

For hundreds of years thereafter, Judah and Israel were each ruled by separate kings.

Moses was a hero—there is no doubt about that. But he was a tragic hero, in the classic sense: a great man brought down by a fatal flaw in his own nature.

Within the context of the story, this comes as a surprise. Moses walks with God and thus appears to be invincible. He is triumphant in his struggle with the Pharaoh and the powerful Egyptian army, and during the years of wandering in the Wilderness he successfully keeps the people together, even though they often question his leadership.

During this period, Moses must have been on an internal odyssey as well. And at some point, he seems to have lost his way. For in the end, God denies him the satisfaction of leading the people into the Promised Land.

God does not punish Moses simply because of his own mistakes. As Moses tells the people, "The Lord is angry with me for your sakes." Moses, in other words, must suffer for the sins of the people in general. Again, we have an instance of the Old Testament foreshadowing the New.

When the people of Israel finally do enter the Promised Land, under the leadership of Joshua, they cannot simply settle down to a peaceful existence. They must take the area by military force.

The book of *Joshua* records this military campaign and includes one of the best-known and most intriguing stories in the Bible—the account of the fall of Jericho. According to the sixth chapter of *Joshua*, the Israelites did not immediately attack the city. Instead, carrying the Ark of the Covenant, they marched around the perimeter of the city for seven days. On the seventh day, when the priests blew their trumpets, and the people let out a "great shout," the walls of the city came tumbling down.

There is archaeological evidence to suggest that the walls of Jericho, which date back to 8,000 B.C., did indeed come a-tumblin' down. Whether they were knocked flat by an earthquake, or by the collective primal shout of God's chosen people, we cannot say. It is a wonderful story, nevertheless—and it is a fitting way to mark the triumph of a people who had come so far, and struggled so long, since Abraham first wandered out of his homeland at God's behest.

Over the next millenium, the people of Israel would enjoy many more triumphs and experience many more setbacks. At times they would be close to God—and at times they would turn their backs on Him.

But always, there would be signs of hope. Among the most noteworthy is the prophecy of Isaiah: one day, he promised, a savior would be born. "He shall be called the Prince of Peace, and of his kingdom there shall be no end."

The Adoration of the Magi. c. 1624. Peter Paul Rubens. Royal Museum of Fine Arts, Antwerp.

chapter 7

The Word Made Flesh

L ike the stories of the Old Testament, the stories of Jesus' birth, life, death and resurrection emerged from oral traditions. Christ's earliest disciples simply moved around the region telling people of his ministry. Scholars believe that the first Gospel wasn't written before about 70 A.D., and that the other three were developed sometime in the course of the next three decades. But in the years since, there has been more ink—and blood—spilled over this man than over any other human being in history.

Given the impact that Jesus has had on our culture, it is difficult to imagine a time when he wasn't widely known. But during his lifetime, his activities would not have been noteworthy to a lot of people. After all, like Moses, he was a man of extremely humble origins. As an adult, he made a name for himself in Palestine. But he was probably one of many wandering preachers in the region.

In the long run, of course, he proved to be much more than just another preacher. Through the efforts of four apostles, whom we know by the names Matthew, Mark, Luke and John—as well as a fifth named Paul—Jesus eventually became the focal point of a new world religion.

The Annunciation

In the beginning was the Word, and the Word was with God, and the Word was God. All things were made by Him and without Him was nothing. In Him was life; and the life was the light of men.

He came in the world and the world was made through Him, and the world did not know Him. He came to His own, and His own did not receive Him.

So the Word became flesh and dwelt among us, full of grace and truth; the only Son of the Father: Jesus Christ.

Now the birth of Jesus was this way:

In the days of Herod, the king of Judea, the angel Gabriel was sent from God to a town in Galilee, named Nazareth, to a maid espoused to a man named Joseph; and the maiden's name was Mary.

And the angel came to her, and said, "Hail, the Lord is with thee: blessed art thou among women."

And when she saw him she was troubled.

But the angel said, "Fear not, Mary: for thou hast found favor with God. Behold, thou shalt conceive in thy womb and bring forth a son and call his name JESUS. And of his kingdom there shall be no end."

Betrothal of the Virgin. 1504. Raphael. Pinacoteca di Brera, Milan.

And Mary said, "Behold the handmaid of the Lord: be it according to thy word."

And the angel departed.

And Mary said, "My soul does magnify the Lord. And my spirit has rejoiced in my Savior.

"Behold, henceforth, all generations shall call me blessed. For He that is mighty hath done to me great things; and holy is His name.

"He has put down the mighty, and exalted them of low degree. He has filled the hungry with good things in remembrance of His mercy. To give light to them that sit in darkness and in the shadow of death, to guide our feet in the way of peace."

The Birth of Jesus

Now it came to pass in those days, that there went out a decree from Caesar Augustus, that all the world should be counted. And all went to be tallied, every one to his own city. Joseph also went up from Galilee, out of Nazareth into Judea, to the city of David called Bethlehem, to be counted with Mary his wife, who was great with child.

And so it was that, while they were there, the days were accomplished that she should be delivered. And because there was no room for them in the inn, she brought forth her firstborn son, wrapped him in swaddling clothes, and laid him in a manger.

Now there were in the same country, shepherds abiding in the field, keeping watch over their flock by night. And lo, the angel of the Lord came upon them, and the glory of the Lord shone round them; and they were sore afraid.

But the angel said to them, "Fear not; for behold, I bring you good tidings of great joy, which shall be to all men. For unto you is born this day, in the city of David, a Savior, which is Christ the Lord.

OVERLEAF: *Adoration of the Child.* 17th century. Gerrit van Honthorst. Galleria degli Uffizi, Florence.

"And this shall be a sign to you. Ye shall find the babe wrapped in swaddling clothes, lying in a manger."

And suddenly there was with the angel a multitude of the heavenly host, praising God and saying, "Glory to God in the highest, and on earth, peace, good will toward men!"

And as the angels were going away from them into heaven, the shepherds said one to another, "Let us go to Bethlehem, and see this thing which is come to pass, which the Lord hath made known to us."

Then, behold, there came wise men, saying, "Where is he that is born King? For we have seen his star in the East, in Bethlehem." And lo, the star went, before them all, till it came and stood over where the young child was. When they saw that, they rejoiced.

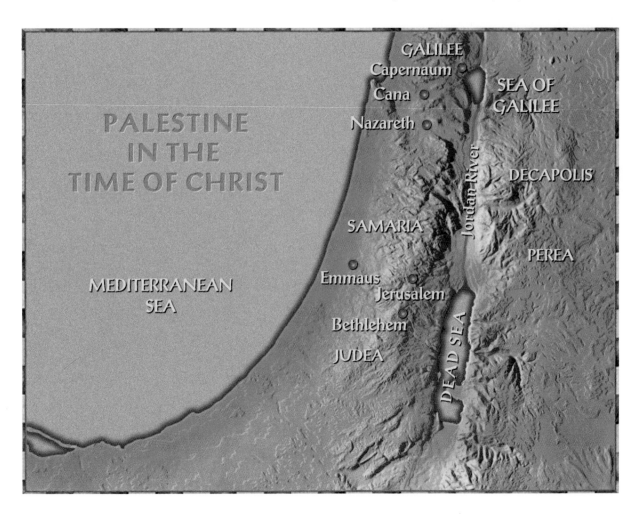

Adoration of the shepherds. Early 15th century. Robert Campin. Musée de Dijon.

And they came with haste, and found Mary and Joseph and the babe, lying in a manger.

And they fell down and worshipped him. Then they opened their treasures, and gave to him gifts of gold and frankincense and myrrh.

And when they had seen him, they made known abroad what was told them of this child.

And all that heard them wondered at these things.

And the shepherds returned, glorifying and praising God. And when they departed, behold, the angel of the Lord appeared to Joseph in a dream, saying, "Arise, and take the child and his mother, and flee into Egypt, and be thou there until I bring thee word: for King Herod will seek the child and kill him."

So Joseph arose and took the child and his mother by night, and departed into Egypt. But when he was

The Flight to Egypt (detail). 1305-1306. Giotto di Bondone. Scrovegni Chapel, Padua.

in Egypt, behold, the angel appeared again in a dream, saying, "Arise and go back to the land of Israel: for he who sought the child's life is dead."

So, with the child and his mother, he came back to Israel. And he dwelt in the city of Nazareth, so that which was spoken by the prophets might be fulfilled: He shall be called a Nazarene.

Now there was a man in Jerusalem, who was just and devout, named Simeon. And the Holy Ghost was

The Massacre of the Innocents.
c. 1610-1611. Guido Reni.
Pinacoteca, Bologna.

upon him. Thus it was revealed that he should not see death before he had seen the Christ.

And he came into the temple when the parents brought in the child Jesus to do for him after the custom of the law. Then he took him up in his arms, and said, "Lord, now let thy servant depart in peace; for mine eyes have seen thy salvation. A light to the glory of the people of Israel."

And Joseph and his mother marveled.

So the child grew and waxed strong in spirit, filled with wisdom, for the grace of God was upon him.

Now his parents went every year to Jerusalem at the feast of the Passover. And when he was twelve years old, they went, after their custom. But when they had fulfilled the feast, as they returned, the child Jesus tarried behind in Jerusalem; and Joseph and his mother knew not of it.

OPPOSITE: *St. Joseph and the Infant Christ.* c. 1670-1685. Giovanni Battista Gaulli, called Baciccio. Norton Simon Museum, Pasadena.

LEFT: *Madonna and Child.* 1480. Giovanni Bellini. Metropolitan Museum of Art, New York.

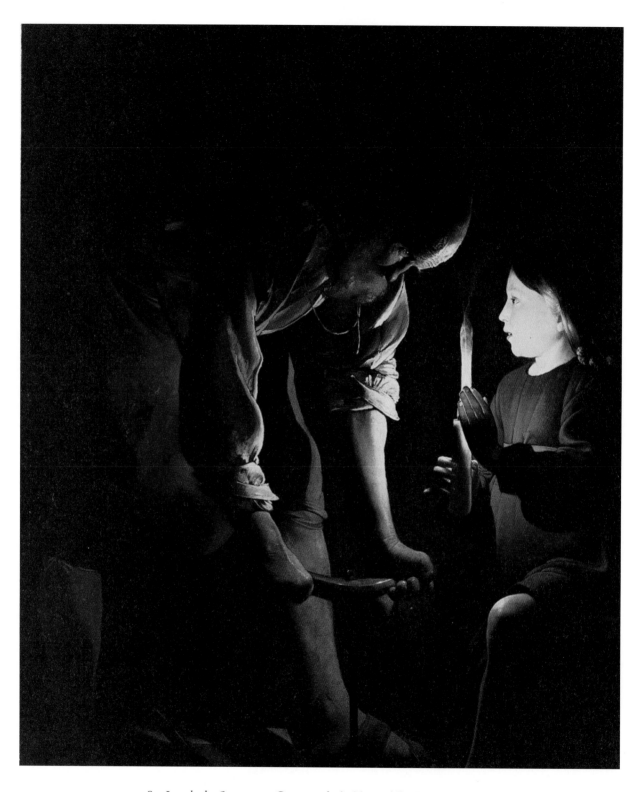

St. Joseph the Carpenter. Georges de la Tour. The Louvre, Paris.

But supposing him to have been in the company, they went a day's journey; and thought him among their kinsfolk and friends.

And when they found him not, they turned back again to Jerusalem, seeking him. So it came to pass, that after three days, they found him in the temple, sitting in the midst of the scholars, both hearing them and asking them questions. And all that heard him were astonished.

And his mother said to him, "Son, why hast thou dealt thus with us? Behold, thy father and I have sought thee, sorrowing."

And he said to them, "How is it that ye sought me? Know ye not that I must be about my Father's business?"

And they understood not what he spoke to them.

But he went with them to Nazareth, and was still a son to them.

So Jesus increased in favor with God and man.

BELOW: *Christ in the House of His Parents.* 1849-1850. Sir John Everett Millais. Tate Gallery, London.

OVERLEAF: *Finding the Savior in the Temple.* 1854-1860. William Holman Hunt. Birmingham City Art Museum, Birmingham.

"So the word was made flesh and dwelt among us, full of grace and truth." But "the world did not know him . . . and understood him not."

Jesus must surely have been an enigma to the people around him, including his own earthly parents. Even as a boy, he seems to have been aware of his destiny. In the story of Jesus in the synagogue, we get a glimpse of his own personal vision. "How is it that ye sought me?" he asks his mother. "Know ye not that I must be about my Father's business?" It is a startling remark, indeed, coming from a twelve-year-old. The scholars in the temple must also have been struck by the apparent precociousness of young Jesus of Nazareth as he sat among them and questioned their teachings.

The writers of the Gospels want us to understand, of course, that Jesus wasn't simply challenging authority in the same way that ordinary young people have throughout history. He was following a path that had been laid out before him. And yet, unlike the figures of the Old Testament, Jesus seems to have acted without direct verbal instructions from God the Father. Instead, he relied on the Holy Spirit—the divine force within him.

Later, as he began preaching and performing miracles, he promised people that if they sincerely embraced the Word of God, they too could share in the power of the Spirit.

Youth of Our Lord. 1847-1856. John Rogers Herbert. Guildhall Art Gallery, London.

Christ Calling Peter and Andrew. 1481-1482. Domenic Ghirlandaio. Sistine Chapel, Vatican.

chapter 8

Preaching the Gospel

Throughout the four Gospels, God the Father speaks primarily through Jesus. But on two occasions, we actually hear the voice of the Almighty. The first is immediately after John the Baptist encounters Jesus on the banks of the River Jordan. It is a dramatic moment indeed.

When Jesus comes to John to be baptized, John protests. He knows who Jesus is and feels that Christ should be baptizing him. Nevertheless, he complies with Jesus' request. As Jesus rises from the water, "the heavens are rent asunder," and a voice calls out, "Thou art my beloved son; in thee I am well pleased." From here on, within the context of the story, there is no doubt about Jesus' special relationship with God.

Later, Jesus' faith in his unique relationship with the Father allows him to meet Satan without fear. The story of their encounter is called the Temptation of Christ, because Satan literally offers the world to Jesus if only he will renounce God. For any normal mortal the offer would be hard to resist. But Jesus never falters. He knows his mission, and he is not about to depart from it—even for all the riches on earth.

The Baptism of Jesus

Now in those days, when Jesus was about thirty years of age, there came John, the Baptist, preaching all around about Jordan, with the voice of one crying in the wilderness, "Make ye ready the way of the Lord! Make his path straight!

"Every valley shall be filled, and every mountain and hill shall be brought low. The crooked shall become straight and the rough way smooth. And men shall see the salvation of God!"

The Baptism of Christ. 15th century. Piero della Francesca. National Gallery of London.

The River Jordan, where Christ is said to have been baptized.
The term "baptism" is derived from a Greek word meaning "to
wash with water." In the Old Testament, washing symbolizes
moral cleansing. The book of Jeremiah, for example, contains the
exhortation, "O Jerusalem, wash thine heart from wickedness." In
the New Testament, the practice is ritualized when crowds follow
John the Baptist to the River Jordan to confess their sins. Jesus is
baptized not for the purpose of washing away sins, but instead as
a prelude to the revelation of His divinity. Today, Christian baptism
symbolizes not only redemption of the soul, but a union with Christ.

ABOVE: *St. John the Baptist Preaching.* Late 17th to early 18th century.
Giovanni Baciccio. The Louvre, Paris.

OPPOSITE: *John the Baptist.* 1509-1512. Leonardo da Vinci. The Louvre, Paris.

And the people wondered in their hearts about John, whether he were the Christ.

But John answered them, "I indeed baptize you, but he that comes after me is mightier than I. After me comes a man who was before me, and I knew him not; whose sandal strap I am not worthy to loosen. He shall baptize you with the Holy Spirit."

And Jesus came from Galilee to John, to be baptized in the Jordan.

John hindered him, saying, "Comest Thou to me? I need to be baptized by Thee."

But Jesus answered, "Suffer it still, for it thus becomes us."

The Voice of One Crying in the Wilderness

The voice of one crying in the wilderness: Prepare the way of the Lord . . .

— ISAIAH 40:3

John the Baptist is among the most important figures in the New Testament. Indeed, when John begins to preach, some people wonder if he is the Messiah. And to King Herod, who has John beheaded, Jesus and John are indistinguishable. Upon learning of Jesus' ministry, Herod says, "This is John the Baptist; he is risen from the dead."

John, of course, draws a sharp distinction between himself and the Son of God. But, as usual, Jesus has the final word: "Among those born of woman," Jesus says, "there has not arisen one greater than John the Baptist; but he who is least in the kingdom of heaven is greater than {John}."

The Baptism of Christ. Late 16th century. Jacopo Tintoretto. San Rocco, Venice.

So Jesus was baptized. And as he came up from the water, the heavens were rent asunder, and a Voice came, saying, "Thou art my beloved Son. In thee I am well pleased."

Temptation in the Wilderness

Then Jesus, full of the Holy Spirit, was led from Jordan into the wilderness, to be tempted by Satan. He was there forty days and forty nights, and ate nothing.

Then the Tempter came to him, saying, "If thou be the Son of God, command this stone that it become bread!"

And Jesus answered him, "It is written that man shall not live by bread alone, but by every word of God."

So Satan brought him to Jerusalem, and set him on a pinnacle of the temple, and said to him, "If thou be the Son of God, cast thyself down from here. For it is

The Monastery of St. George, built at the foot of the cliff where Jesus is said to have been tempted by Satan.

The Temptation of Christ (detail). Sandro Botticelli. Sistine Chapel, Vatican.

written, He shall give his angels charge over thee, to keep thee; and in their hands they shall bear thee up, lest thou dash thy foot against a stone."

And Jesus answered, "It is said, Thou shalt not tempt the Lord thy God."

Then the devil, taking him up to a high mountain, showed him all the kingdoms of the world, in all their glory, in one moment of time. And the Devil said, "To thee will I give all this! That power is mine and to whomsoever I will, I give it; if thou therefore wilt worship me, all shall be thine."

And Jesus said to him, "Get thee behind me, Satan: It is written, thou shalt worship the Lord thy God, and him only."

Then the devil departed, and behold, angels came and ministered unto Jesus. And he returned in the power of the Spirit into Galilee; and there went out a fame of him through all the region. And he taught in the synagogues, being glorified by all.

Rejection in Nazareth

From that time Jesus began to preach, and to say, "Repent, for the kingdom of heaven is at hand."

And he came to Nazareth, where he had been brought up: and, as was his custom, he went into the synagogue on the Sabbath day, and stood up to read.

And he was given the book of the prophet Isaiah. When he opened it, he found the place where it was written, "The Spirit of the Lord is upon me, because He hath anointed me to preach the gospel to the poor; He hath sent me to heal the broken-hearted, to preach deliverance to the captives, and recovering of sight to the blind, to set free them that are bruised, to preach the acceptable year of the Lord."

And all wondered at these words.

And they said, "Is not this Joseph's son? Is not this

The Sea of Galilee. Christ's first apostles were fishermen. He subsequently turned their occupation into a symbol, saying, "I will make you fishers of men."

the carpenter; the son of Mary, the brother of James, and Joseph of Juda, and Simon? And are not his sisters here with us?" They were offended.

But Jesus said to them, "A prophet is not without honor, but in his own country, and among his own kin, and in his own house."

Now in the synagogue there was a man possessed by the spirit of an unclean devil, who cried out with a loud voice, "Let us alone; what have we to do with thee? Thou, Jesus of Nazareth?! Art thou come to destroy us? I know thee who thou art; the Holy One of God!"

But Jesus said, "Hold thy peace, and come out of him." And the devil threw the man down, and came out of him, and hurt him no more.

And they were all amazed, saying, "What a word is this! He commands the unclean spirits, and they come out. Can it be that they know him for the Christ?!"

So the fame of him went round about, into every place.

Now, when the sun was setting, all that were sick

came to him; and he laid his hands on every one, and healed them. And when it was day, he departed into the desert. The people sought to stay him, that he should not leave them.

But he said, "I must preach the kingdom of God to other cities also; for therefore am I sent."

The Calling of the Disciples

And he preached in the synagogues of Galilee.

And passing by the sea of Galilee, he saw Simon, and Andrew his brother, casting a net into the sea; for they were fishers.

The Miraculous Draught of Fishes. Early 16th century. Raphael. Victoria and Albert Museum, London.

And Jesus said to them, "Come ye after me, and I will make you fishers of men!" And they left their nets and followed him.

Then another came, and said, "Knowest thou me?"

And Jesus said, "I saw thee, before, when thou wast under a fig tree."

And the man said, "Thou are truly the Son of God."

Then Jesus answered, "Because I said I saw thee under a fig tree, believest thou? Verily, thou shall see greater things than these."

And to another he said, "What seek ye?"

And the man answered, "We have found him."

So Jesus said, "Come, follow me."

He called unto him whom he would, and they went. And of these disciples, he chose twelve: Simon, whom he called Peter, and Andrew his brother; James and John, Philip and Bartholomew; Matthew and Thomas; James, the son of Alphaeus, and Simon called Zelotes. And Judas, the brother of James, and Judas Iscariot, who also was the traitor.

The Sermon on the Mount

Now there came great numbers that were troubled, from all Judea, to hear him and be healed. And they were healed.

So the multitude sought to touch him, or even the hem of his garment, such power came from him.

Then he came down with them, and stood on a level place, on a mountain, with his disciples. And he lifted his eyes, and said:

"Blessed are the poor in spirit, for theirs is the kingdom of God.

"Blessed are they that mourn, for they shall be comforted.

"Blessed are the merciful, for they shall obtain mercy.

"Blessed are they that hunger now; for they shall be
     filled.

"Blessed are they that weep now; for they shall laugh.

"Blessed are the meek; for they shall inherit the earth.

"Blessed are the peacemakers; for they shall be
     called the children of God.

"And blessed are ye, when men shall hate you, and
     cast your name as evil, for my sake.

"Rejoice in that day, for so did they unto the
prophets.

"But woe unto you, when all men shall speak well
of you! For so did they to the false prophets.

"Woe unto you that laugh now; for ye shall mourn
and weep. Woe unto you that are full now, for ye shall
hunger.

"Think not I came to destroy the law, or the
prophets. I came not to destroy but to fulfill.

"So I say unto you which hear, Love your enemies,
do good to them which hate you. Bless them that curse
you, and pray for them that ill-use you.

"Ye have heard it said, 'An eye for an eye, and a
tooth for a tooth.' But I say to you, That ye resist not
evil. Whosoever shall smite thee on the right cheek,
turn to him the other also. Give to every man that asks
of thee; and of him that taketh away thy goods ask
them not back again.

"And as ye would that men should do to you, do ye
also to them. For if ye love those who love you, what
thanks have ye? Sinners also love those that love them.

"And if ye do good to them of whom ye hope to
receive, what thanks have ye? Sinners do even the same.
But love your enemies, and do good, hoping for nothing in return, and your reward shall be great; then ye
shall be the children of God.

"Be ye mercifiul as your Father is merciful. Judge not,
and ye shall not be judged; condemn not, and ye shall not
be condemned; Forgive, and ye shall be forgiven.

OVERLEAF: *Sermon on the Mount.*
1481-1482. Cosimo Rosselli.
Sistine Chapel, Vatican.

"Give, and it shall be given unto you; good measure, running over. For with the same measure you use, it shall be measured unto you."

And he spoke to them in parables, saying, "Can the blind lead the blind? Shall not both fall into the ditch?

"How can Satan cast out Satan? A corrupt tree cannot bring forth good fruit. So by their fruits shall ye know them. Do men gather grapes from thorns, or figs from thistles?

"A good man out of the good treasure of his heart brings forth good; and an evil man brings forth evil.

"Straight is the gate, and narrow is the way, that leads to eternal life, and few there be that find it.

"And I say to you truly, I am the door. Seek, and ye shall find. Knock and it shall be opened to you.

"If your son shall ask bread of any of you that is a father, will ye give him a stone? If ye know how to give to your children, how much more shall your Heavenly Father give.

"Therefore I tell ye, do not worry about your life, what ye shall eat, or what ye shall drink.

"Behold the fowls of the air; they neither sow nor reap nor gather into barns, and yet your heavenly father feeds them. Are ye not much better than they?

"And why take ye thought about clothing? Consider the lilies of the field, how they grow; they neither toil nor spin, yet I tell you, even Solomon in all his glory was not arrayed like one of these. If God so clothes the grass of the field, which is alive today and tomorrow is thrown into the oven, shall He not much more clothe you, O ye of little faith?

"Your heavenly Father knows that ye have need of all these things. But seek ye first the kingdom of God, and his righteousness, and all these things shall be given unto you as well.

"And when ye pray, be not like those that stand on the streets and pray in repetitions, and think they shall be seen by men. But enter into thine inmost chamber, and pray to thy Father, after this manner:

"Our Father, which art in Heaven. Hallowed be Thy name.

"Thy Kingdom come, Thy will be done, on earth as it is in heaven.

"Give us this day, our daily bread.

"And forgive us our trespasses, as we forgive those that trespass against us.

"And lead us not into temptation, but deliver us from evil.

"For Thine is the Kingdom, and the power and the glory, for ever and ever. Amen."

Then a woman in the crowd lifted her voice and said, "Blessed is the womb that bore thee!"

The map below shows sites where Jesus is believed to have preached and performed miracles. Scholars do not know with certainty that these events took place at these particular sites.

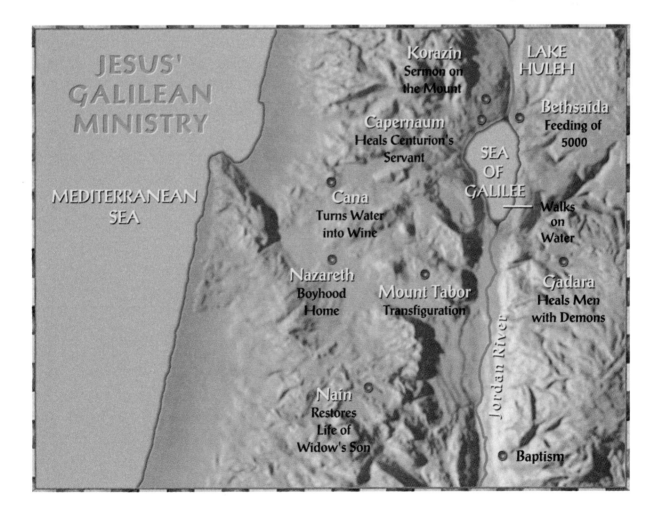

The dictionary defines "parable" as "a short allegorical story designed to convey a truth or moral lesson."

The parables of Jesus range from short aphorisms—or one-liners—to longer stories containing many different symbols. An example of the former is Jesus' well-known comment that "If a blind man leads a blind man, both will fall into a pit." Clearly, Jesus is not speaking literally about the dangers of the blind leading the blind. He is using blindness as a metaphor for a lack of moral and spiritual vision.

The most famous of the longer parables is the story of the prodigal son. In this tale, the son who leaves home and squanders his father's money is intended to represent the person who turns his back on God. When he realizes the error of his ways, he is forgiven in the same way that God forgives repentant sinners.

But he said, "Yea, rather blessed are they that hear the word of God and keep it. Why call me 'Lord! Lord!' yet not do the things that I say?

"Hear then the parable of the sower. Behold the sower went forth to sow, and as he sowed, some seeds fell on rocky places, and the birds came and devoured them.

"Thus, when anyone hears the word of the Kingdom of God, and understands it not, then cometh the Evil one, and snatches away that which hath been sown in the rocky places of his heart.

"But he that hears the word, and understands it, he verily bears fruit in his heart a hundredfold. Take heed, therefore, how ye hear, for so is the Kingdom of God. As if a man should cast seed upon the earth and sleep and rise, night and day, and the seed springs and grows, he knows not how.

"If ye say, 'What is the Kingdom of God like?' I say unto you, it is like a grain of mustard seed cast into a garden, where it grows into a great tree. And the birds of the air lodge in its branches.

"Therefore, whoever heareth these words and does them, I liken him unto a wise man, who built his house upon a rock. And the rain descended, and the floods came and the winds blew, and beat upon that house; and it fell not; for it was founded upon a rock."

And when Jesus had ended so, then there came his brethren and his mother; and, waiting nearby, they sent to him. Where the multitudes sat about him and the people said to him, "Behold thy mother and thy brethren seek for ye."

But he answered, "Who is my mother, or my brethren! For whosoever shall do the will of God, he is my brother, and my sister, and my mother!"

Go and Sin No More

Then Jesus went from there and came into the coasts of

Judea by the far side of Jordan. And again there came to him great multitudes, and again he taught them. And they brought young children to him, that he should touch them: and his disciples rebuked them.

But when Jesus saw this, he was much displeased. He said to them, "Suffer the little children to come unto me. Forbid them not; for of such is the Kingdom of God.

"Verily, I say unto you, except ye turn and become as little children, ye can in no way enter the kingdom."

And he took the children up in his arms, and laid his hands upon them, and blessed them, and said, "Whosoever shall receive this little child in my name receiveth me; and whosoever receiveth me, receiveth not me, but Him that sent me."

And there were the lame, the blind, the dumb, and the maimed: they fell down at his feet, and he healed them, and all wondered to see the dumb speak and the maimed whole; the lame walk and the blind see.

And his disciples, seeing Jesus heal one, who had been blind from his birth, said, "Good Master, who did sin? This man, or his parents, that he was born blind?"

And Jesus said, "Why callest thou me good? There is none good but one; that is God.

"Neither this man nor his parents sinned. This was so the hand of God should be made manifest in him. I must do the work of Him that sent me, while it is day; the night cometh, when no man can work."

Then came certain Pharisees, and they said to him who had been blind, "How were thine eyes opened?"

He answered, "By a man called Jesus. He said to me, 'Go to the pool of Siloam, and wash'; and I went and washed, and I see." Then they said, "This man is not of God because he keepeth not the Sabbath day, for it was the Sabbath."

They said, "What sayest thou of him that he hath opened thine eyes?" He said, "He is a prophet."

Then they said, "Give God the praise. We know

OVERLEAF: *Parable of the Blind.*
c. 1568. Pieter Brueghel.
Museo Nazionale, Naples.

that this man is a sinner."

He answered, "Whether he be a sinner, I know not. One thing I know is that I was blind and now I see."

But they said again, "What did he to thee?"

He answered them, "I have told you already, wherefore would ye hear it again? Will ye also be his disciples?"

Then they said, "Thou art his disciple. As for this fellow, we know not from whence he is."

The man said, "Why here's a marvellous thing, ye know not from whence he is, and yet he has opened mine eyes. Since the world began, never was it heard that any man opened the eyes of one that was born blind!"

Now Jesus heard and said to them, "I am the light of the world. He that followeth me shall not walk in darkness."

Jesus came again to the temple, early in the morning, and the people came to him, and he sat down and taught them.

And then the Pharisees brought in a woman, and sat her before him, and said, "Master, this woman was taken in adultery, in the very act. Now Moses, in the Law, commanded us that such should be stoned. But what sayest thou?"

And Jesus leaned down and wrote in the ground with his finger, as though he heard them not. When they asked him again, he looked up and said, "Let him that is without sin among you cast the first stone."

And they went out, every one. And Jesus was left alone with the woman. He said to her, "Woman, where now are thy accusers? Hath no man condemned thee?"

She said, "No man, Lord." And Jesus said, "Neither do I. Go, and sin no more."

The dictionary defines "sermon" as "a religious discourse delivered in public by a clergyman as part of a religious service." Jesus wasn't a clergyman, and he didn't speak at formal services—although you could call him a rabbi, which means "teacher." I think "Sermon on the Mount" seems the wrong title too. It reads to me more like a big open camp meeting. Must've been quite a crowd, though: "great numbers, from all Judea," it says. They're beginning to hear about this new young rabbi, so they come, and are amazed and uplifted by his message.

This is the richest time of teaching for Jesus. With his disciples, he roams all over Judea, "spreading the Word," much as the circuit-riding preachers did in rural America up through the early decades of this century.

Jesus didn't simply preach, of course. He also performed miracles as a way of emphasizing the power of faith. Miracles abound in the Old Testament as well, but the context is different. When God, acting through Moses, parts the Red Sea, the event is witnessed by thousands. Christ's miracles, by contrast, are often witnessed by a mere handful of people. This seems entirely appropriate, of course, given Jesus' profound humility. He claims to speak the Truth, to be sure. But ultimately he points away from himself toward the Father. "Why callest thou me good?" he asks. "There is none good but one; that is God."

The Transfiguration. 1487. Giovanni Bellini. Museo Nazionale di Capodimonte, Naples.

chapter 9

The Light of the World

As the story of Jesus' ministry unfolds, it becomes clear that he is aware of his fate. But he is not fearful. On the contrary, he appears to have no attachment whatsoever to the material world. Moreover, he continually urges his disciples not to worry about physical dangers. His message is summed up beautifully in the paradoxical remark, "For whosoever would save his life shall lose it, and whosoever shall lose his life for my sake, shall find it."

Elsewhere, he is more straightforward: "Do not fear those who kill the body but cannot kill the soul," Matthew quotes him as saying. "Rather fear him who can destroy both soul and body in hell." In the early chapters of the Gospels, which are filled with messages of love and hope, warnings like these seem to strike suddenly, out of nowhere, like serpents. But the Gospels' later chapters contain darker passages still: dire warnings of a time when "nation will rise against nation," and the earth will be consumed by pestilence.

In the end, he says, the Son of Man will come in glory to reward the faithful. But he can't say when this will happen. And therein lies the drama.

And they went forth from thence, through Galilee, where he would not that any man should know him. For the Pharisees had said, "Get thee hence from here; for Herod will kill thee!"

But Jesus answered, "Here must I walk still. Today, and tomorrow, and the days following. For I know whence I came, and whither I go, but ye know neither whence I came nor what I do."

Though he spoke these words, no man took him because his hour had not yet come.

Nonetheless, many of the multitudes turned back, and walked no more with him.

But Jesus marked it not, because he knew from the beginning who they would be that believed not, and also who would betray him.

RIGHT: *Christ Entering Jerusalem, The Maestà Altarpiece.* c. 1308-1311. Duccio di Buonisegna. Museo dell'Opera del Duomo, Siena.

OPPOSITE: *St. Peter.* Leonardo da Vinci. Graphische Sammlung Albertina, Vienna.

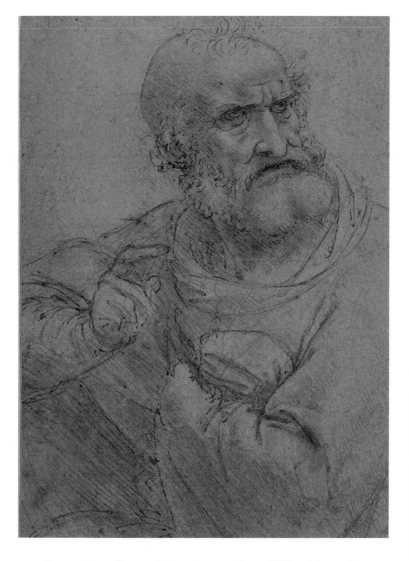

OVERLEAF: *Christ's Charge to St. Peter.* Raphael. Victoria and Albert Museum, London.

Jesus therefore said to the twelve, "Would ye also go away?"

Simon Peter answered, "Lord, to whom shall we go? Thou hast the words of life. Thou art the Christ."

And Jesus smiled and said, "And thou art Peter. Upon this rock will I build my church.

"Unto thee will I give the keys of the Kingdom— and even death shall not prevail against it."

He told his disciples how he must go into Jerusalem, saying to them, "The Son of Man shall be delivered into the hands of man."

They understood not, but they were afraid. And Jesus said to them, "Foxes have holes and the birds of

ABOVE: *Jesus Giving the Keys to St. Peter.* Jean-Auguste-Dominique Ingres. Ingres Museum, Mintaulan.

OPPOSITE: *Christ Driving the Money Changers Out of the Temple.* c. 1625. Rembrandt van Rijn.
Pushkin Museum of Fine Arts, Moscow.

heaven have nests, but the Son of Man hath nowhere to lay his head.

"If any man would come after me, let him leave all, and take up his cross and follow me."

Then Peter said, "Lo, we have left all, we have followed thee."

Jesus answered, "There is no man that hath left house or brethren, or sisters, or father, or mother, or wife, or children, for my sake, but he shall receive eternal life in the world to come.

"But many that are first shall be last; and the last shall be first. For whosoever would save his life shall lose it, and whosoever shall lose his life for my sake, shall find it.

OVERLEAF: *Christ Driving the Merchants from the Temple.* c. 1650. Jacob Jordaens. The Louvre, Paris.

"And what shall a man get for his life?"

So when at last they had come unto Jerusalem, all the city was moved, saying "Who is this?"

"This is Jesus, the prophet of Nazareth of Galilee."

And Jesus went into the temple of God and cast out all of them that sold and bought in the temple. He overthrew the tables of the moneychangers, and the seats of them that sold doves.

And he said to them, "It is written, my Father's house shall be called the house of prayer; yet you have made it a den of thieves!"

A Vision of the Apocalypse

And as he went out from the temple, one of his disciples said, "Behold, how it is adorned with goodly stones."

And Jesus said, "As for these things, behold, the day will come; there shall not be left one stone upon another; all shall be thrown down."

And they asked him, "Master, but when shall these things be? And what sign shall there be?"

And Jesus sighed deep in his spirit, and said, "Why do ye seek a sign? Verily, I say to you, there shall be no sign. When ye see a cloud rise out of the west, ye say, there comes rain, and so it is. And when ye see the south wind blow, ye say there will be heat, and so it comes.

"Ye can read the signs of the sky and the earth. How is it ye cannot read the signs of this time?

"Suppose ye that I am come to give peace on earth? I tell you NO, but rather division.

"There shall be houses divided. Son against father, and father against son. And ye shall hear of wars and rumors of wars; for all these things must come to pass; but the end is not yet.

"For nation shall rise against nation, and kingdom

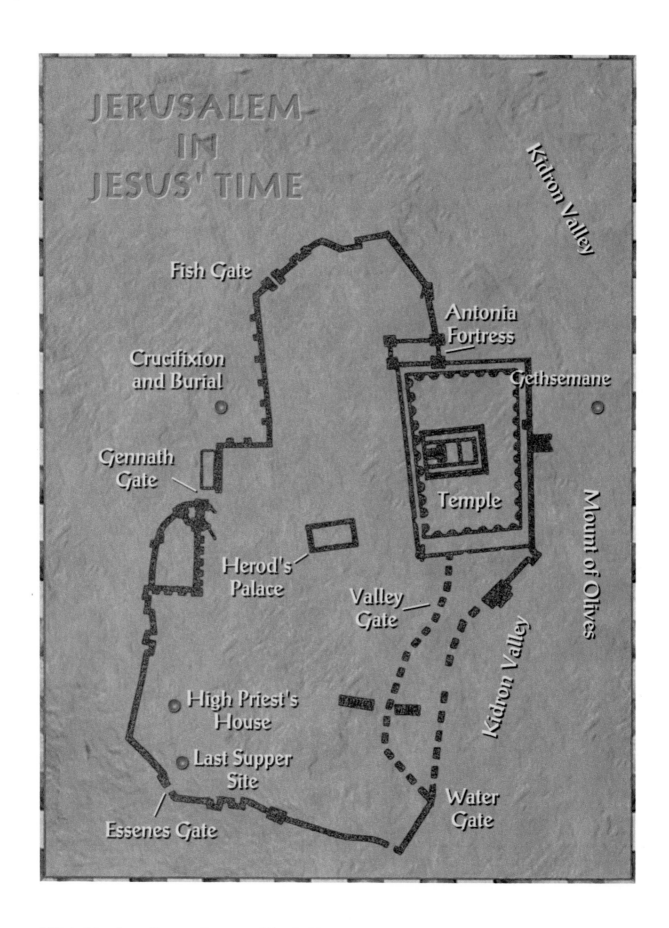

JERUSALEM
IN
JESUS' TIME

Kidron Valley

Fish Gate

Antonia
Fortress

Crucifixion
and Burial

Gethsemane

Gennath
Gate

Temple

Mount of Olives

Herod's
Palace

Valley
Gate

Kidron Valley

High Priest's
House

Last Supper
Site

Water
Gate

Essenes Gate

against kingdom: and there shall be famines and pestilences, and earthquakes. All these are the beginning of sorrows.

"O Jerusalem, Jerusalem, ye kill the prophets and stone them which are sent to thee. I would have gathered thy children together, and ye would not!

"Behold, your house shall be left desolate. And ye shall not see me, until the time comes when ye shall say, 'Blessed is he that cometh in the name of the Lord.'

"Take ye heed! Behold, I have foretold you all things.

"And in those days, after that tribulation, the sun shall be darkened, and the moon shall not give her light. The stars of heaven shall fall, and then shall they see the Son of Man coming in clouds with glory, and a great sound of a trumpet.

A quiet moment on the Mount of Olives, overlooking Jerusalem.

Christer and the Virgin (detail), The Last Judgement. 1535-1541.
Michelangelo Buonarotti.
Sistine Chapel, Vatican.

"And then shall he send his angels, and shall gather all nations from the four winds, from the uttermost part of the earth. And all shall be before him.

"Then shall the Son say, 'Come ye blessed of my Father, inherit the kingdom prepared for you from the foundation of the world: For I was hungry, and ye gave me meat. I was thirsty, and ye gave me drink! I was a stranger, and ye took me in; naked, and ye clothed me. I was sick, and ye visited me. I was in prison, and ye came to me.

"Then shall the righteous say, 'Lord, we did not these things unto thee.'

"And the Son shall answer them, 'Inasmuch as ye have done this unto one of the least of my brethren, ye have done this to me.'

"Take heed! I say, when all these things be done, Heaven and earth shall pass away; but my words shall not pass away.

"But of that day and that hour knowest no man. No, not the angels in heaven. Therefore take heed, watch and pray; for ye know not when the time is. The Son of Man is as a man taking a far journey, who left his house and gave to every man his work and his watch.

"Watch ye therefore; for ye know not when the master cometh; at even, or at midnight; at cockcrow, or in the morning. And what I say unto you I say unto all: Watch."

The "Wailing Wall," Jerusalem.

Jesus' entry into Jerusalem marked a transition in his ministry: the period of quiet preaching in the countryside had passed. It was time to venture into the city.

Jerusalem, at the time, was already filled with religious radicals. Their presence posed a problem for both the Roman governor—a man named Pontius Pilate—and the priests of Israel, since challenges to the status quo created varying degrees of unrest among the people.

To the priests, Jesus was becoming especially troublesome. By storming into the Temple, and overturning the tables of the moneychangers, he was issuing a very public challenge to the religious authorities.

The scene in the Temple cannot be fully appreciated unless you understand the historical context. Devout Jews were forbidden to pay the Temple tax with Roman coins because those coins had graven images on them. The moneychangers provided worshippers with plain coins—for a fee, of course. Jesus does not appear to have been opposed to this pratice, per se. But he was outraged over the fact that it was taking place inside the Temple. To him, it was one more sign of the degeneracy of the times.

The priests, needless to say, saw things differently. From their perspective, the moneychangers were performing a necessary service. In any event, it was not the place of some itinerant preacher from a marginal town called Nazareth to question the practice. Something would have to be done.

Christ Lamenting Over Jerusalem. 1842. Sir Charles Eastlake. Glasgow Art Gallery.

The Institution of the Eucharist. 1647. Nicolas Poussin. The Louvre, Paris.

chapter 10

Behold, The Hour Cometh

Disturbed by Jesus' effect on people, the priests try to have him arrested. But their first attempt fails. Jesus is so charismatic, it seems, that even the officers sent to capture him cannot bring themselves to lay hands upon him. Later, when asked to explain their actions, the officers answer simply: "There never was a man who spoke so."

What exactly do they mean by this? Certainly, people were struck by Jesus' ideas about God and the conduct of life. But they were also struck by the unusual way in which he expressed those ideas. Jesus was a masterful communicator, indeed. Thus when spies sent by the Pharisees attempt to entrap him with incriminating questions, they are easily foiled.

"Is it right to pay taxes to Caesar?" they ask, assuming that Jesus will deny Caesar's authority. But Jesus surprises them: "Render unto Caesar the things that are Caesar's, and unto God the things that are God's," he says. The time will come when Jesus will choose to remain speechless in the face of his accusers. But the time for his surrender has not yet come.

The Symbolism of the Lamb

Behold, I send you forth as lambs in the midst of wolves.

Luke 10:3

When Jesus likens his disciples to lambs among wolves, he is not simply suggesting that their work will be dangerous. Throughout the Bible, lambs represent sacrifice. In Genesis 22, for example, Abraham tells Isaac that "God will provide for Himself the lamb for a burnt offering."

Later in the Bible, when Isaiah predicts the coming of the Savior, he says that the Messiah will be "led as a lamb to slaughter." (Isaiah 53:7)

The most important reference to lambs in the New Testament comes in John 1:29. When John the Baptist sees Jesus coming, he says, "Behold, the Lamb of God, who taketh away the sins of the world." In other words, just as ancient Hebrews literally offered sacrificial lambs to God, Jesus would offer himself as a "sacrificial lamb" to atone for the sins of mankind. The disciples were not to be sacrificed in the sense that Jesus was. But, they endured persecution in the name of Christ, and, in that sense, sacrificed themselves for mankind.

Murmuring Among the Multitudes

Now there was much murmuring among the multitudes concerning Jesus. Some said, "He is a good man," and others said, "Nay, he leads the people astray."

But still, Jesus went up into the temple and taught, saying, "My teaching is not mine, but His that sent me. If any man wills, he shall know whether I be of God, or whether I speak for myself."

Some therefore said, "Is this he whom they seek to kill? Lo, he speaks openly, and they say nothing to him. Can it be that the rulers know that this is the Christ?"

But some answered, "We know whence this man is; but when the Christ cometh, no one knows whence he is."

Jesus said, "Ye know me, and know whence I am; but I am not come of myself but from him whom ye know not."

Now the Pharisees heard the multitude murmuring, and the chief priests sent officers to take him where he stood. But when they heard him cry, "If any man thirst let him come unto me and drink," some of these men said, "This is truly a prophet. This is the Christ."

Still, others said, "What, doth the Christ come out of Galilee? Hath not the scripture said that the Christ cometh out of Bethlehem?"

Still, no man would lay hands on him. The chief priests said to them, "Why did ye not bring him? Are ye also led astray?"

The officers answered, "There never was a man who spoke so."

Now after this, Jesus appointed other disciples and sent them two and two into every city and place.

And he said to them, "The harvest is at hand, but the laborers are few. Therefore, go your ways. Yet beware; I send you forth as lambs in the midst of wolves.

"Still, into whatever city ye enter, say to them, 'The Kingdom of God is nigh.' I send you to tread upon serpents and scorpions; yet nothing shall hurt you, for your names are writ in heaven."

The Conspiracy of the Pharisees

Now the feast of unleavened bread drew nigh, which is called the Passover, and many went up out of the country to Jerusalem to purify themselves. They asked there for Jesus in the temple, saying, "What think ye?

OPPOSITE: *Head of Christ.* 1495. Leonardo da Vinci. Pinacoteca di Brera, Milan.

Tribute Money. Tomas Masaccio. Santa Maria del Carmine, Florence.

That he will not come?" For the priests had commanded that if any man knew where he was, he should tell it, that they might take him.

So the Pharisees took counsel how they might do this. And they sent forth spies, saying, "Master we know thou art true, and teachest the way of God, and carest not for anyone. Tell us therefore; what thinkest thou? Is it lawful to give tribute unto Caesar, or not?"

But Jesus said to them, "Why are you trying to entrap me? Show me a coin." When they brought him a coin he said, "Whose is this image and superscription?"

And they said, "Caesar's."

And he said, "Then render unto Caesar's the things that are Caesar's, and unto God the things that are God's."

So they held their peace, and went on their way.

Now, since the Passover was at hand, the priests and the scribes and the elders of the people gathered together in the palace of the high priest, who was called Caiaphas, and consulted how they might take Jesus by craft, and kill him. But they said, "Not on the feast day, lest a tumult arise among the people."

Now Jesus was in Bethany at this time in the house of Simon the leper. And, as he sat down to eat, the woman Mary Magdalene came with an alabaster box of precious ointment and poured it on his head.

When Judas Iscariot saw this, he said, "To what purpose is this waste? This ointment might have been sold for much money to give to the poor." And they

Mary Magdalene: detail from Noli me Tangere. c. 1534. Antonio Correggio. Museo del Prado, Madrid.

Judas and the Thirty Pieces,
The Maestà Altarpiece.
c. 1308-1311. Duccio di
Buonisegna. Museo dell'Opera
del Duomo, Siena.

all murmured against her.

But Jesus said to them, "Why trouble ye the woman? She hath wrought a good work.

"The poor ye have always with you; but me ye have not always. She hath poured this ointment for my burial. And I say, verily, wheresoever this gospel shall be preached, in the whole world, there shall also this be told, what this woman hath done."

Then Satan entered into Judas, though he was one of the twelve, and he went away to the chief priests. And he said to them, "What will ye give me, if I deliver him to you?" And they weighed and gave him thirty pieces of silver.

And from that time on he sought to betray Jesus to them.

The Last Supper

Now the first day of the feast, the disciples did as Jesus had appointed them, and made ready the Passover.

And when it was evening, he came with the twelve and sat at meat. And as they did eat, Jesus rose from supper, and took a towel and girded himself. Then he poured water and began to wash the disciples' feet, and to wipe them.

So he came to Peter, who said, "Lord, thou shall never wash my feet!"

Christ Washing Peter's Feet. 1852-1856. Ford Madox Brown. The Tate Gallery, London.

The Institution of the Eucharist

The question of whether the Last Supper was a Passover meal, or a gathering shortly before Passover, remains unanswered. The fourth Gospel suggests the latter; the first three imply the former.

For Christians, of course, the question is secondary. What is important is that the meal eventually became the basis for the institution variously known as the Lord's Supper, Holy Communion, or the Holy Eucharist. (The word eucharist comes from the Greek eucharista, *meaning "thanksgiving.")*

The celebration is interpreted differently by different denominations. The Roman Catholic Church teaches that the bread and wine are miraculously transformed into Christ's body and blood during the ceremony. Others believe that the bread and wine retain their basic substance but that the spirit of Christ is present in the sacraments. In any event, two thousand years after the death of Christ, the celebration of the eucharist remains central to the faith of millions of people.

Jesus answered, "If I wash thee not, thou hast no part with me. What I do, thou knowest not now; but thou shalt hereafter. Ye are clean, but not all are clean."

So he sat down again and said, "Know ye what I have done? Ye call me, 'Master' and 'Lord' and ye say well; but still I say to you that one of you shall betray me. His hand is with me on this table."

The twelve looked one on another, doubting and said to him one by one, "Lord, is it I?"

And he answered, "He that dips his hand with me in this dish, the same shall betray me.

"The Son of Man goeth as it is written."

Then Judas said, "Master, is it I?"

And Jesus answered, "Thou hast said. What thou doest, do quickly."

Now no man at the table knew what he spoke to Judas, who went out straightaway; and it was night.

When he was gone, Jesus said, "Children, yet a little while I am with you. So now, a new commandment I give unto you; that ye love one another, even as I have loved you. By this shall all men know ye."

Peter then said, "Lord, whither goest thou?"

Jesus answered, "Whither I go thou canst not follow."

Peter said, "Lord, why can I not follow thee? I will lay down my life for thee."

Jesus answered, "Wilt thou lay down thy life for me? First sit down and count the cost.

"Ye know not what ye ask."

Peter said, "Even if I must die with thee, I will not deny thee."

And Jesus answered, "Verily? Verily, I say to thee, the cock shall not crow till thou hast denied me thrice.

"For I say, this which is written must be fulfilled."

OPPOSITE: *The Last Supper (detail).* c. 1445-1450. Andrea del Castagno. S. Appolonia, Florence.

BELOW: *The Last Supper.* 1495-1498. Leonardo da Vinci. Santa Maria delle Grazie, Milan.

OVERLEAF: *The Sacrament of the Last Supper.* 1955. Salvador Dali.

The Last Supper (detail),
The Maestà Altarpiece.
c. 1308-1311. Duccio di
Buonisegna. Museo dell'Opera
del Duomo, Siena.

And so he took bread and blessed and broke it, and gave it to them and said, "Take, eat. This is my body, which is given for you. Do this in remembrance of me."

And he took the cup and gave thanks and gave it to them, saying, "This is my blood of the new testament, which is shed for you." And they all drank of it.

But Jesus said to them, "I will no more drink of the fruit of the vine until that day that I drink it new in the kingdom of God. But let not your heart be troubled. In my Father's house are many mansions; if it were not so, I would have told you. And if I go, I come again; that where I am, there ye may be also."

Thomas said to him, "Lord, we know not whither thou goest; how know we the way?"

Jesus said, "I am the way, and the truth and the life: no one cometh unto the Father but by me."

Philip said, "Lord, show us the Father."

Jesus said, "Have I been so long with you, and dost thou not know me, Philip? I am the Father; ye know Him; He abides with you. I will not leave you desolate. Yet a little while and the world beholds me no more; but ye behold me: because I live, ye shall live also.

"Let not your heart be fearful. If ye love me, rejoice because I go!

"And now I have told you. I will speak with you no more, for the world cometh. Arise, let us go hence, that the world may know that I love the Father."

And when they had sung a hymn, they went out to the Mount of Olives. Then Jesus said to them, "Behold, the hour cometh; yea it is come, that ye shall be scattered, every man, and leave me alone.

"In the world ye shall have tribulation: but be of good cheer; I have overcome the world."

The Last Supper (detail).
1445-1450. Andrea del
Castagno. S. Appolonia,
Florence.

Many stories in the Bible deal with loyalty and betrayal, but none does so more directly than the account of Christ's last Passover meal with his disciples.

Having taken thirty pieces of silver in exchange for a promise to deliver Jesus into the hands of the priests, Judas has set himself on a course from which there is no turning back. He will be known throughout history as a betrayer.

I can't help wondering why Judas would do such a thing. The story says he was momentarily overtaken by Satan. Still, there must also have been some human motive at work. Was it mere money that Judas was after? Or was he afraid of the religious authorities? Perhaps all of these forces were at work. After all, if there is one thing the Bible teaches us, it is that we humans are not simple creatures. We often must wrestle with a variety of conflicting feelings. And in moments of weakness, it is easy to justify our own moral transgressions, just the way Judas must have.

Peter, by contrast, seems certain of his loyalty and of his virtue. "I will lay down my life for thee," he tells Jesus. But Christ knows better. He does not doubt that Peter *feels* loyalty. But he seems to recognize that his disciple is speaking in a moment of idealistic passion. He knows that, in the end, Peter's human weaknesses will get the best of him.

Christ in the Garden of Olives. Eugene Delacroix. Eglise St. Paul-St. Louis, Paris.

Christ on the Way to Calvary. 1566. Jacopo Tintoretto. Scuola Grande di San Rocco, Venice.

chapter 11

The Son of Man Is Taken

In his letter to the Philippians, the apostle Paul writes that Christ was both "equal with God" and "made in the likeness of man." Jesus' dual nature is what makes the Gospels so interesting. At times he seems to completely transcend his own humanity. But as the story approaches its climax, he seems very human indeed.

While he awaits the arrival of Judas, for instance, he prays "in agony" and great drops of sweat fall to the ground. He is not afraid, certainly. But he is suffering, nonetheless. That should not surprise us, of course. Christ's ability to suffer—to feel human pain—is crucial to the Gospels. It is what gives the story of the crucifixion its resonance.

A short time later, when Christ rises from his prayers to find his disciples sleeping, he seems downright irritated. "What?" he asks. "Could ye not watch with me one hour?" But before long, he regains his sense of calm. After praying again, he smiles on his disciples and forgives them for their weakness. "Sleep on now," he says. "The hour has come."

Jesus and his disciples came to a place which was named Gethsemane, and he said to them:

"Abide ye here while I pray. And watch." And he went forward a little and fell on the ground and said, "O my Father, if thou be willing take away this cup from me. Nevertheless, not what I will, but what thou wilt be done!"

And in an agony he prayed, and his sweat was as great drops of blood falling down to the ground. And

Agony in the Garden.
Andrea Mantegna. National Gallery, London.

The Garden of Gethsemane, on the Mount of Olives, where Christ

is said to have gone to pray on the night he was betrayed. The garden

is mentioned by name in Matthew 26:36 and in Mark 14:32.

Luke does not mention a garden of any kind but does mention Jesus'

praying on the Mount of Olives. John, on the other hand, provides no

account of Jesus' praying before his betrayal, but suggests that the

betrayal itself took place in a garden. No one knows for sure whether

this is, in fact, the garden in which Jesus prayed. Authenticity has

been claimed for several other sites in the area as well.

as he rose up from prayer, he came to his disciples and found them sleeping. And he said to Peter, "What, could ye not watch with me one hour? The spirit is indeed willing, but the flesh is weak."

And again he went away and prayed, and spoke the same words. And when he returned he found them asleep again, for their eyes were heavy. And he said to them, "Sleep on now, take your rest. It is enough, the hour is come. Behold, the Son of Man is taken."

The Kiss of Judas, The Maestà Altarpiece. c.1308-1311. Duccio di Buonisegna. Museo dell'Opera del Duomo, Siena.

And while he spoke, Judas came and with him a band of soldiers, with swords and torches.

Jesus therefore went forth and said, "Whom seek ye?"

They answered, "Jesus of Nazareth." And Judas came to him and said, "Hail, Master," and kissed him.

And Jesus said, "Friend, do that for which thou art come." Then they came and laid hands on him and took him.

Now Peter had a sword and drew it, and struck the high priest's servant. But Jesus said to Peter, "Put up thy sword. This cup the Father has given to me. Shall I not drink it?"

So the chief captain bound him.

And Jesus said to him, "Are ye come out to take me as a thief, with swords? When I was daily in the temple, you stretched forth no hand against me. But this is your hour. And this is done."

Then all the disciples forsook him, and fled.

The Trial of Jesus

Now they led Jesus away to Caiaphas, the high priest, and Peter followed afar off. And they brought him even into the palace of the priests, where were assembled all the elders and scribes.

But Peter was standing without, in the court. And when the servants had kindled a fire, he sat with them and warmed himself.

Then the chief priests and all the council sought witness against Jesus to put him to death.

But they found none.

Then at last came two false men, swearing, "This fellow said, 'I can destroy the temple of God and build it in three days.'"

And the high priest arose and said to him, "Answerest thou nothing? What is it which these men witness against thee?"

OVERLEAF: *The Denial of St. Peter (detail).* c. 1620-1625. Gerrit van Honthorst. Minneapolis Institute of the Arts.

But Jesus held his peace. So the high priest said, "I command thee by the living God, that thou tell us. Art thou the Christ?"

And Jesus said, "Ye say that I am: why ask thou me? Ask them that have heard me; they know the things which I said."

Then the high priest said, "What, need we any further witnesses? We ourselves have heard from his own mouth. Ye have heard the blasphemy. What think ye?" They answered, "He is worthy of death!"

Then the men that held Jesus spit in his face and mocked him; and others blindfolded him, and struck him saying: "Prophesy unto us, oh Christ, which is he that struck thee?"

Now Peter still sat without, warming himself, when a maid came to him, saying, "Art thou a disciple of this Jesus?"

And he denied, saying, "I know not what thou sayest."

And another maid saw him and said to them that were there, "This fellow was also with the Nazarene."

And with the oath, he denied again: "I know not the man."

After awhile, another that stood by said to Peter, "Surely thou art one of them, for thou art a Galilean; thy speech betrays thee!"

But Peter swore, "Man, I am NOT!"

And at once the cock crowed. Then Peter remembered the words of Jesus: "Before the cock crows, thou shalt deny me thrice." And he went out and wept.

Then Judas, when he saw that Jesus was condemned, repented and brought back the thirty pieces of silver to the priests, saying, "I have sinned: I have betrayed innocent blood."

And they said, "What is that to us? See thou to that."

So he threw down the pieces of silver in the temple and went away and hanged himself.

When the morning was come, all the chief priests and elders of the people took counsel against Jesus to put him to death. And when they had bound him, they led him away and delivered him up to Pontius Pilate.

Pilate said to them, "What accusation bring ye against this man?"

They answered, "If this man were not an evil doer, we should not have delivered him up to Rome."

Pilate said, "Take him yourselves and judge him according to your law."

The priests said, "It is not lawful for us to put any man to death. But we found this fellow perverting the nation and forbidding to give tribute to Caesar, saying that he himself is Christ, a King."

And Pilate asked him, "Art thou the King of the Jews?"

And Jesus answered, "Thou sayest that I am a king. To this end am I come into the world, that I should bear witness unto the truth."

And Pilate said to him, "What is the truth?"

Now again, the priests accused Jesus.

So Pilate again asked him, "Answerest thou nothing? Behold how many things they accuse thee of."

But Jesus answered no more: not even one word; so the governor said to the priests, "I find no fault in this man."

But they were all the more urgent, saying, "He stirs up the people throughout all Judea!"

Now at this feast the governor was wont to release to the people one prisoner, whomsoever they would.

So Pilate called together the priests and the people also. And he said to them, "Ye brought me this man, and having examined him before you I find no fault in him. Nothing worthy of death has been done by him. I will therefore chastise him and release him for your Passover.

"Will ye that I release to you this King of the Jews?"

Now there was one named Barabbas, who had made rebellion, and for this, and for murder, lay bound in prison.

The Governor said to them, "Which of the two would you wish I release to you?"

Now the priests moved the people, so they cried out, "Barabbas!"

Pilate said, "What shall I do then with Jesus?"

And they all cried, "Let him be crucified!"

Then Pilate said, "Why? What evil has he done?"

But they cried out the more, "CRUCIFY HIM!" And these voices prevailed.

So Pilate, to content the people, released Barabbas, whom they asked for, and delivered Jesus up to their will. The soldiers took him and scourged him. And they plaited a crown of thorns and put it on his head, and arrayed him in a purple garment.

Then they brought him out again and Pilate said to the people, "Behold, the man!"

But they cried out as before, "Away with him, away with him! Crucify him!"

When Pilate said, "Shall I crucify your King?" they answered "We have no king but Caesar!"

And they mocked Jesus, saying "Hail, King of the Jews!"

So they took the robe from him and led him away to crucify him. Jesus went out bearing the cross for himself, but as they led him on the way, they took hold of one Simon of Cyrene and laid the cross on him, to bear it after Jesus.

And a great company of people followed him, and women also, bewailing and lamenting.

But Jesus, turning to them, said, "Daughters of Jerusalem, weep not for me. Weep for yourselves, and for your children. For the days are coming when they shall say, 'Blessed are the barren and the wombs that never bore and the breasts that never nursed.' Then shall they say to the mountains, 'Fall on us'; and to the

BELOW: *Christ Carrying the Cross.* c. 1517-1592. Jacopo Bassano. Musée des Beaux Arts, Quimper.

OPPOSITE: *Christ on the Way to Calvary (detail).* 1566. Jacopo Tintoretto. S. Rocco, Venice.

*For centuries, the word "cru-
cifixion" has been associated
almost exclusively with
Christ. But in Jesus' day,
crucifixion was a common
method of torture and execution.*

*The practice was especially
common in times of war,
according to Jouette M.
Bassler, professor of New
Testament Theology at Southern Methodist University in
Dallas, Texas. At times,
thousands of victims would be
posted on stakes as a way of
intimidating the people of
besieged cities.*

*Eventually, the ritual
came to include practices that
are associated with Jesus'
death: flogging, parading the
victim to the execution site,
and nailing the victim to a
cross.*

*The practice continued long
after Jesus' death, though it
was not always carried out in
the same manner. There were,
for example, many different
types of crosses. St. Andrew is
said to have been nailed to an
X-shaped cross, while St.
Peter is reported to have been
crucified upside down, at this
request, because he did not feel
worthy to die in the same way
that Christ had.*

hills, 'Cover us.' For if they do these things in a green
time, what shall they do in a dry?"

And when they were come to a place called
Golgotha, that is to say, the place of the skull, they gave
him wine to drink mingled with gall. When he tasted
it, he would not drink.

Then they crucified him.

And Jesus said, "Father, forgive them; for they know
not what they do." Then they that crucified him took
his garments and cast lots to decide what every man
should take.

And with him they crucified two thieves; the one on
his right hand, and the other on his left. And now it
was the third hour. And they set up over his head a sign
which read: "THIS IS THE KING OF THE JEWS."

Now many read this, for the place where Jesus was
crucified was near the city, and it was written in
Hebrew and in Latin and in Greek. The priests there-

Via Dolarosa, Jerusalem. Each year, devout Christians commemorate Christ's journey to the cross by walking this route.

fore said to Pilate, "Write not, 'The King of the Jews' but that he said 'I am the King of the Jews.'"

Pilate answered, "What I have written, I have written."

And the people stood and watched him there. Also the elders, nodding their heads and saying, "He saved others; himself he cannot save. If he be the King of Israel, let him now come down from the cross and we will believe him."

And one of the thieves which were hanged railed against him, saying, "If thou be Christ, save thyself and us."

But the other rebuked him, saying, "Dost thou not fear God? We received due reward for our deeds; but this man has done nothing."

And he said to Jesus, "Lord when thou comest into thy kingdom, remember me!"

Jesus answered, "I say to thee, today shalt thou be with me in paradise."

Standing by the cross of Jesus were his mother, and his mother's sister, and Mary Magdalene.

Now it was about the sixth hour, and a darkness came over the whole land until the ninth hour, the sun's light failing.

And about the ninth hour Jesus cried with a loud voice, "My God, my God, why hast Thou forsaken me?"

Then he said, "It is finished," and cried, "Father, into Thy hands I commend my spirit."

And having said thus, he gave up the ghost.

OVERLEAF: *Calvary.* 1456.
Andrea Mantegna.
The Louvre, Paris.

This story—like all great drama—is filled with irony. Just think about it. You have the Son of God—the most exalted man on earth—nailed to a cross between two common criminals. And you have a group of priests who, in trying to destroy him, made him infinitely more powerful than they could have ever imagined.

There is much irony elsewhere in the Gospels as well. It is reflected in scenes such as the one in which Jesus—the heir to the throne of David—rides into Jerusalem on a lowly donkey. And it can be found in Jesus' sayings, such as "The last shall be first."

But perhaps the most ironic moment in the entire Bible comes at the end of the story of the crucifixion. "It is finished," Jesus cries out. He is referring to his mission on earth. But in a larger sense, this moment is more a beginning than an end. Jesus has died. But by doing so, he has overcome death and granted mankind the promise of eternal life.

Christ on the Cross. 1835.
Eugene Delacroix.
Musée de la Cohue, Vannes.

The Ascension of Christ. Rembrandt van Rijn. Alte Pinakothek, Munich.

chapter 12

He Is Risen

The story of the resurrection is the heart of the New Testament. Having delivered his message to mankind—and accepted the burden of their sins—Jesus comes back from the grave.

He has several reasons for doing so, it seems. His immediate concern is to reassure his disciples and to forgive Peter for denying association with him. More important, however, is his desire to provide reliable living witnesses to his resurrection and to inspire his disciples to spread the Word, which he has given them.

All four Gospels describe these events in detail—and with great dramatic effect. Whether they actually happened is, of course, neither provable nor disprovable. But perhaps that is the point. It is within our nature to remain skeptical in the absence of concrete evidence, just as the apostle Thomas did when he was first told of the resurrection. But Christ's early followers eventually realized that such skepticism must be overcome. As St. Paul says in his second letter to the Corinthians, "We live by faith, not by sight."

*Throughout history, the num-
ber three has had symbolic
importance. Indeed, to the
Greek philosopher Pythagoras
it represented divine perfec-
tion. That idea is reflected
in the Christian concept of
the Trinity and in the fre-
quent apperance of the number
throughout the Bible.*

*

*In Matthew 12:40, Jesus
predicts the duration of his
burial with reference to
another Biblical story incor-
porating the number three:
"For as Jonah was three days
and three nights in the
whale's belly, so shall the Son
of Man be three days and
three nights in the heart of the
earth."*

*

*In the first letter of John (not
to be confused with the fourth
Gospel), the apostle states,
"there are three that testify:
the Spirit, the water and the
blood."*

*

*Other important references
to the number three appear
in Genesis 6:10, Exodus
23:14, Proverbs 30:29,
Ecclesiastes, and Corinthians.*

The Resurrection

Now the sun was darkened and the veil of the temple was rent in twain from top to bottom. And when the centurion that stood by over all saw what was done, he said, "Truly this was a righteous man."

And all the people that came together there smote their breasts and cried. And all that followed him from Galilee, and the women, stood afar off, beholding these things.

And now, when the even was come, because it was the day before the Sabbath, a man named Joseph of Arimathaea, a good man, and righteous, who also had been a disciple, came and went in boldly to Pilate and asked for the body of Jesus.

And Pilate gave him leave.

So Joseph brought fine linen and took Jesus down

from the cross and wrapped him in the linen and laid him in his own new tomb, which was hewn out of a rock; and he rolled a great stone to the door of the tomb.

And Mary Magdalene and Mary, the mother of Jesus, and the Mary also who came with him from Galilee beheld the sepulchre, and how his body was laid. And they returned and prepared spices and ointments; and rested on the Sabbath day, according to the commandment.

Descent from the Cross.
Rogier van der Weyden.
c. 1435. Museo del Prado,
Madrid.

Now as it began to dawn, on the first day of the
week, they came to the sepulchre at the rising of the
sun. And they said among themselves, "Who shall roll
us away the stone from the door?" But when they
looked, they saw that the stone was rolled away. And
entering the tomb, they saw an angel sitting on the
right side. His appearance was as lightning, and his
garment white as snow.

And he said to them, "Why seek ye the living
among the dead? Jesus the Nazarene, who was crucified, is risen. He is not here! Come, see the place where
the Lord lay!

"So go your way, tell his disciples that he goeth
before you! But ye shall see him, as he told!"

And they remembered his words and returned from the sepulchre and told all these things unto the eleven.

Then Peter arose and ran unto the sepulchre; and stooping down, he beheld the linen clothes laid by themselves; and he wondered in himself at that which was come to pass.

Then went in also another disciple. And he saw and believed. Then the disciples went away again unto their home.

But Mary Magdalene stood still at the sepulchre, weeping. And as she turned, she saw Jesus standing there, but she knew him not. Supposing him to be the gardener, she said, "They have taken away my lord; I know not where they have laid him."

And Jesus said to her, "Mary, whom seekest thou?"

And she said, "Master!"

So he said to her, "Mary, touch me not, but go to my

BELOW: *The Church of the Holy Sepulchre, Jerusalem, built on the site where Christ is said to have been entombed.*

OVERLEAF: *The Angel Opening the Sepulchre of Christ (detail).* 17th century. Albert Cuyp. Museum of Fine Arts, Budapest.

brethren and say I ascend unto my Father and your Father, to my God and your God."

And she went and told the disciples that she had seen the Lord and what he had spoken.

But one of them, Thomas, said, "Unless I see in His hands the print of the nails, and put my finger there, I will not believe."

So that evening, Jesus came where the disciples were and stood among them and said, "Peace be with you." And to Thomas he said, "Reach hither thy finger; behold, my hands."

When morning came, Jesus stood on the shore: but the disciples knew not that it was Jesus.

Then Jesus said, "Children have ye any food?"

They answered that they did not.

Then Jesus said unto them, "Cast the net on the right side of the ship, and ye shall find some."

They did as they were told and now they were not able to draw in their net because of the multitude of fishes it contained.

The disciple whom Jesus loved said, "It is the Lord!"

Jesus said unto them, "Bring the fish which ye have now caught."

And when they had dined, Jesus said to Simon Peter, "Simon, son of John, lovest thou me?"

Peter answered, "Yea, Lord, thou knowest that I love thee."

And Jesus said to him, "Tend my sheep."

Then to all he said, "As the Father has sent me, even so I send you. Go ye into all the world and preach the gospel to the whole creation!"

Jesus' Appearances After the Resurrection

The four Gospels offer various accounts of Jesus' appearances after his resurrection. One interesting story is found in Luke 24: 13-32. *The story begins with the risen Christ appearing to two of the disciples as they are walking toward the village of Emmaus.*

Initially, the disciples do not recognize Jesus and they begin to talk to him as if he is a stranger, telling him of their bewilderment over the empty tomb.

"O fools," Jesus says, telling them that they are "slow of heart to believe all that the prophets have spoken: Ought not Christ to have suffered these things, and to enter into his glory?"

Later, they sit down to supper with Christ, still unaware of who he is. Finally, when Christ breaks bread, and blesses it, "their eyes are opened." Immediately thereafter, Jesus vanishes.

oward the end of *The Gospel According to John,* Jesus imparts the power of the Holy Spirit to his disciples by breathing on them. And so, the Bible comes full circle, back to the point in *Genesis* when God first breathed life into Adam. The difference, of course, is that Jesus is granting eternal life.

Later, the author of *John* tells us that there are many stories of Jesus' ministry which were never recorded. Alas, he says, a full account of Jesus' life and teachings would require more books than could be contained in all the world.

The New Testament does contain other writings besides the Gospels, of course. There is *The Acts of the Apostles,* which describes the spread of Christ's message after his death and resurrection. (Historians believe *Acts* was written by the same man who wrote *The Gospel According to Luke.*) There are the wonderful letters of *Paul* who, by his own admission, opposed followers of Christ until he experienced a conversion and became the most important evangelist of all. There are a handful of letters by other apostles. And, finally, there is the vivid, apocalyptic vision of *The Revelation of St. John The Divine.*

Today, nearly two millennia after the death of Jesus, mankind remains captivated by the words contained in these books. The longevity of these writings is a testament to their power. It seems that Jesus was right when he predicted before his disciples, "My words shall not pass away."

*A wall amidst the ruins of a first-century Roman amphitheater in
Israel. Three centuries after the death of Christ, Christianity
became the dominant religion within the Roman Empire.*

Now of the things
which Jesus did,
if they should
be written every one,
I suppose that even
the world itself
could not contain
the books that would
be written.

—*The Gospel According to St. John 21:25*

The Four Evangelists.
c. 1625. Jacob Jordaens.
The Louvre, Paris.

THE RISE OF CHRISTIANITY TO 125 A.D.

Pergamos (Pergamum)
Thyatira
Smyrna
Philadelphia
Ephesus
Sardis
Laodicea

London
Cologna

Lyons

Segovia

Cordoba

Rome

BLACK SEA

Byzantium (Constantinople)

Philippi

Puteoli

Thessalonica

Tarsus

Athens

Antioch

Sicily

Corinth

Salamis

Carthage

Damascus

MEDITERRANEAN
SEA

Jerusalem

KEY

Cyrene

⊙ Early Christian Community

Alexandria

RED SEA

⊙ One of Seven Churches of Asia
(See Revelation 1:11)

⊙ Part of the Roman Empire

Afterword

In the decades immediately following the Crucifixion, Christ's disciples continued to teach in the same way that Jesus himself had taught—by preaching and telling stories. In fact, it is believed that the first Gospel—generally thought to be *Mark*—was not written until about 70 A.D. Most scholars agree that *Matthew* and *Luke* were written fifteen or twenty years later and that *John* was produced around the end of the first century. Still, the oral tradition remained strong, and it would be several centuries before anyone would combine these writings with the books of the Old Testament to form the Christian Bible as we know it.

We do know that the writings of the Old Testament had existed in various forms centuries before Christ was born. In fact, while no one knows exactly when the sacred stories of the ancient Israelites were first written down, scholars have determined that a Greek translation of the Hebrew Bible—known as the Septuagint—was produced in Alexandria during the third century B.C. The Dead Sea Scrolls, discovered in 1947 in Wadi Qumran, near the northwest shore of the Dead Sea, have shed additional

Charlton Heston at Wadi Qumran, where the Dead Sea Scrolls were discovered in 1947.

light on the development of the Bible. The scrolls—which predate all other such documents by at least a thousand years—include the Hebrew texts of almost every story in the Old Testament.

Before a Christian Bible could be produced, followers of Christ would have to agree on which writings should be included. During first three centuries A.D., there appears to have been widespread disagreement over which Christian writings were authoritative. In the second century, for example, there were some Christians who accepted only the *Gospel of Luke* and a few of *Paul*'s letters. This is rather remarkable, given that many Christian writings had been produced by this point.

As long as Christianity remained a minor sect, such disagreements would inevitably continue. In the fourth century A.D., however, the Roman Emperor Constantine the Great embraced Christ as the Messiah, and Christianity quickly became the dominant religion within the empire.

In 382 A.D., Pope Damasus issued a definitive list of Old and New Testament books that were recognized by the church. Four years later, he commissioned a monk named Jerome to produce a Latin translation of those books. Because Jerome wrote in contemporary Latin, the new translation was called the Vulgate (or common) Bible. It was copied, re-copied and

A Hebrew Temple Scroll.

carried across Europe, and it heightened the status of the Bible—not only as Scripture, but as literature. Indeed, the translation is considered so important that the Church later bestowed sainthood on Jerome in recognition of his work. After the fall of Rome, Christianity continued to spread. Soon Christian monks began preaching in Britain and, with the support of King Alfred the Great—who ruled from 871 to 899 A.D.—parts of the Bible were translated into the maturing English language.

In spite of these developments, the first complete English translation of the Latin Vulgate Bible was not produced until 1380. The delay was due, in large part, to opposition from the church hierarchy. Church fathers argued that the common man should not have direct access to the Bible— that only priests could properly interpret the Scriptures. (Even St. Jerome is reported to have said, "You can make no progress in the Holy Scriptures unless you have a guide to show you the way.") Thus, when a man named William Tyndale produced the first New Testament from the original Greek in 1525, a bishop burned most of the copies. Some years later, Tyndale himself was executed.

Meanwhile, the status of the Latin Vulgate Edition had been heightened in 1456 when Johann Gutenberg reproduced it on his new printing press. But it was only a matter of time before this extraordinary invention would also be used to reproduce new English translations of the Scriptures.

In 1539, Henry VIII authorized the publication of an edition based in part on Tyndale's work. He called it the Great Bible, and ordered it dis-

ABOVE: *The Four Apostles.* c.1526. Albrecht Duerer. Pinakothek, Munich.

PREVIOUS PAGES: *St. Jerome.* c. 1607. Caravaggio. Museum of the Cathedral of St. John, Malta.

tributed to every church in England, so that "all manner of persons—rich and poor, priests and laymen, lords and ladies, husbands and wives—may learn" from it.

When King James I assumed the throne in 1603, he decided to commission yet another translation of the Scriptures. Classically educated himself, he appointed forty seven scholars to the project. The translators were divided into panels which met separately in Westminster, Oxford, and Cambridge. Each group worked on different sections of the Bible, using both Greek and Hebrew sources as well as existing English translations. When the three panels had completed their work, they sent it to a fourth panel, which wove it all into a final text to be submitted to King James.

The project was worthwhile—to say the least. In 1611, after seven years of effort, the King James Bible was published and became recognized at once as a great work of literature. It has retained this status for nearly 400 years.

In modern times, many other English editions have been produced. The New Revised Standard Edition is among the most recent. And, because of its accessible language, it is also among the most popular. Meanwhile, the Bible has also been translated into many other languages. In fact, according to the Biblical scholar J. R. Porter, it has been published either in whole or in part—in more than *two thousand* foreign languages, representing eighty percent of the world's population.

Through all its many editions, the Bible has had an enormous impact on our literature and our everyday language. Indeed, some of the greatest

Portrait of Henry VIII. c. 1537. Hans Holbein, the Younger.
Galleria Nazionale d'Arte, Antica.

literary works of Western Civilization, such as *Paradise Lost,* are based squarely on the Bible. Other classics, such as the plays of Shakespeare, do not incorporate Biblical themes per se, but, many of the plays are infused with Biblical symbolism and imagery. In *Macbeth,* for example, the famous line "Out, out, brief candle! Life's but a walking shadow . . . ," echoes the book of *Job,* which states that "our days upon earth are but a shadow." The

Bible's influence on American writers has been equally profound. *Moby Dick,* to cite just one example, is laced with allusions to the Books of *Genesis, Job, Jonah* and *Kings.*

The language of the Bible is not just reflected in great books, of course. It has influenced our spoken language as well. When Abraham Lincoln, for example, warned that the institution of slavery had created "a house divided against itself" he was paraphrasing *Luke 11:17.* More than a century later, when Ronald Reagan likened America to "a city upon a hill," he was reviving an idea first put forth by the Puritan leader John Winthrop. The great Puritan leader had, in turn, borrowed the phrase from the New Testament.

Chances are, your own speech is colored by Biblical expressions as well. If you have ever used the word "scapegoat," for example, or commented that someone "can't read the writing on the wall," you have alluded to the Bible—though perhaps without knowing it. (If you'd like to know precisely where these expressions come from, see *Leviticus 16:10* and *Daniel 5:5-8* respectively.)

For millions of people, of course, the Bible's literary merits are secondary. They read the Bible in the way that its authors intended to be read: as the Word of God. But the beauty of the Bible is that it can be profitably read by everyone—archbishops and atheists alike. Regardless of your point of view, I hope this book has helped you to see the Bible in a new light.

A Book-by-Book Summary of the Bible

Although we often think of the Bible as a single book, it is actually a collection of sixty-six separate books.

The Old Testament contains thirty-nine books, which can be divided into categories. The first five—*Genesis, Exodus, Leviticus, Numbers* and *Deuteronomy*—are collectively known to Christians as the Pentateuch and to Jews as the Torah. They are also called The Books of Moses because Moses has traditionally been regarded as their principal author.

The next twelve books, from *Joshua* through *Esther,* are called the historical books. They describe the history of the ancient Israelites, from the conquest of the Promised Land through the restoration of Israel after the Babylonian exile.

The books of *Job, Psalms, Proverbs, Ecclesiastes* and *The Song of Solomon,* are generally categorized as poetical books or wisdom literature. Finally, there are seventeen books of prophecy, beginning with *Isaiah* and ending with *Malachi.* As you read the Bible, it's important to bear in mind that the categories outlined above are not rigid. The historical books contain many prophecies, for example, and historical references are scattered throughout the prophetical books. Moreover, poetic writing can be found in virtually all of the books of the Old Testament. Nevertheless, the categories are helpful for readers who are picking up the Bible for the first time, as well as for those who are studying it in depth.

Genesis

The word "genesis" comes from a Greek word meaning origins, and that, essentially, is what this book is about—the origins of humanity and of the Jewish people. The first eleven chapters of the book deal with mankind in general, from the creation of heaven and earth through the Flood and the dispersion of Noah's descendants around the world. Chapters twelve through fifty tell the stories of the first Hebrew patriarchs—Abraham, Isaac and Jacob.

The stories of the patriarchs are bound together by a single theme: God's promise that the people of Israel will one day have a homeland and will become "a great nation." The final chapters of the book, which tell the story of Joseph in Egypt, reinforce this theme. On his deathbed, Joseph tells his brothers, "God will surely come to you and bring you up out of this land to the land he swore to Abraham and Isaac, and to Jacob." This remark sets the stage for the central story of the next book.

Exodus

While the book of *Genesis* weaves together the stories of many people, *Exodus* focuses on a single character: Moses.

It is useful to think of the book in two parts. The first part describes the oppression of the Israelites under a new Egyptian king "who did not know Joseph," and God's selection of Moses as the man who will liberate the people from bondage. The second part is an account of the Exodus itself. (The word "exodus" comes from a Greek word meaning departure.)

After the crossing of the Red Sea, the Israelites must travel through a vast desert-wilderness. During the journey, God miraculously provides food and water. He also presents to Moses the Ten Commandments and promises that if the people adhere to the Law, they will prosper. Nevertheless, the people constantly complain that the trip is too difficult. Their expressed lack of faith angers God, and He makes it clear that punishment will be sure and swift if they turn their back on Him again.

While *Exodus* contains some of the most exciting stories in the Bible, there is very little action in the latter half of the book. It describes in great detail the construction of the tabernacle, the vestments of priests, rules governing the sacrifice of animals and other esoteric matters. But the book closes with a striking image that symbolizes God's eternal presence among the people: "For the cloud of the Lord was upon the tabernacle by day, and fire was on it by night, in the sight of all the house of Israel, throughout all their journeys."

Leviticus

The title of this book is a reference to the priests of the tribe of Levi, one of Jacob's twelve sons. *Leviticus* has no storyline, per se. Instead, it elaborates on the legal code that was the focus of the latter part of *Exodus*. Specifically, the book focuses on the ritual of sacrifice; the institution of the priesthood; the religious significance of cleanliness, and the practice of holiness.

While many of these laws are no longer relevant, some are as enduring as any in the Bible. In chapter nineteen, for example, we find a commandment that was later underscored by Jesus: "Thou shalt love thy neighbor as thyself."

The other main points of interest in *Leviticus* are those passages, in chapter twenty-three, dealing with the celebration of Passover, Yom Kippur, Rosh Hashanah and other annual feasts.

Numbers

The title of this book refers to the census—or numbering—of the people, which is described in the first few chapters. The purpose of the census is twofold: it will serve as a guideline for military strategy and it will facilitate the allocation of territories after the conquest of the Promised Land.

Much of the rest of the book is an account of the Israelites' journey through the desert. In keeping with the account in *Exodus,* the journey is characterized by constant complaining. As a result of their lack of faith, the people must wander in the desert for forty years.

Deuteronomy

The title of the book means "second law," and it is so named because it repeats the stories and laws contained in *Exodus, Leviticus* and *Numbers.* In chapter five, for example, Moses reviews the Ten Commandments. But because *Deuteronomy* is built around several discourses by Moses, its tone is more personal than that of the earlier books.

Toward the end of the book, Moses explains the blessings that will come as a result of obedience to God and the curses that will follow disobedience. Then, after offering a final blessing to each of the twelve tribes of Israel, Moses climbs Mount Nebo. From this vantage point, he is allowed to look out over the Promised Land but is told by God that he shall not be allowed to enter it. The book ends with Moses' death and the acceptance of Joshua as the new leader of Israel.

Joshua

In the very first chapter of this book, God orders Joshua to lead the people over the Jordan and into Canaan. Moreover, He promises that if Joshua abides by the Law, he will prosper and have "good success."

The story of the crossing of the Jordan, told in chapter three, echoes the account of the crossing of the Red Sea. When the people set foot in the river, the waters are parted by God. The next two chapters serve as a prelude to one of the book's highlights—the story of the fall of Jericho.

The invasion of Jericho, described in chapter six, begins not with a military assault but with an unusual ritual. Led by the priests, who are responsible for carrying the ark, the Israelites march around Jericho's walls for six days. On the seventh day, the people knock the walls down flat with "a great shout." After that, they easily take the city.

In the next battle, at the city of Ai, the Israelites are defeated as a direct result of a sin committed by an individual Israelite. When the sinner is punished, God's good will toward His people is restored, and a string of military victories follows.

The second half of *Joshua* focuses on the allocation of territories of the Promised Land. Nevertheless, there are some very moving passages in the final chapters. Indeed, one of the highlights of the book comes in chapter twenty-three, when Joshua delivers his farewell speech. He warns that pockets of resistance remain throughout the Promised Land and that they will serve "as snares" for God's people.

Judges

After the death of Joshua, according to the book of *Judges,* there arose "another generation . . . which knew not the Lord, nor the works He had done for Israel." Ignorant of their heritage, the people revert to the worship of pagan gods. Needless to say, this angers the Lord.

As punishment, God allows remaining groups of Canaanites, such as the Midianites and the Philistines, to temporarily conquer the Israelites. In fact, this happens several times in the course of the book. In each instance, however, God redeems His people by raising up a leader—or judge—who can liberate them. Among the judges are Deborah, Gideon and Samson.

The story of Samson is especially interesting because, unlike the other judges who rallied large armies, he fights alone. When Delilah, the woman he loves, learns the secret of his legendary strength and reveals it to the Philistines, Samson is rendered helpless. In one last act of revenge, however, he pulls down the pillars of a building where three thousand Philistines are celebrating. Everyone present is killed—including Samson himself.

Ruth

The book of *Ruth* is set in the time of *Judges*, but it does not tell the story of a judge. Ruth is a Moabite woman who is left widowed after her Israelite husband dies. Early in the story, Ruth's father-in-law dies as well, so she returns to Judah with her mother-in-law, Naomi.

Shortly after her arrival, Ruth finds work in the field of a man named Boaz. As it turns out, Boaz is not only a man of wealth and integrity—he is a relative of her late husband. Acting on advice from Naomi, Ruth wins a proposal of marriage from Boaz. Shortly thereafter, Ruth bears a child.

Up to this point, the book appears to be nothing more than a pleasing tale about a group of ordinary people. However, in the last chapter, we learn that Ruth's son eventually became the grandfather of King David.

Samuel 1 and 2

Samuel was the last and greatest of the judges. The first book of *Samuel* opens with an account of his birth to a previously-barren woman named Hannah. As a child, Samuel is given over to a priest named Eli for religious training. It quickly becomes apparent that the Spirit of God is with him.

As an adult, Samuel serves as judge and is revered by the people of Israel. However, when he grows old and announces that his sons will succeed him, the people are unhappy. "Behold," they tell him, "thy sons walk not in thy ways." Instead of another judge, they want a king.

Confused, Samuel turns to God for guidance. The Lord tells Samuel to do what the people ask and leads him to a young man named Saul. After he is anointed, Saul wins a series of battles. But he soon falls from grace, and the Lord instructs Samuel to anoint a young man named David as Saul's replacement.

The remainder of *1 Samuel* and all of *2 Samuel* tell the story of David. Chapter seventeen of *Samuel 1* relates the familiar story of David's battle with a Philistine giant name Goliath. As a result of David's success in that battle—and in a series of military campaigns afterward—he quickly becomes a hero among the people. However, Saul—who has not actually been dethroned—grows jealous and, several times, tries to kill David.

In spite of Saul's hostility toward him, David remains devoted to the king, and when Saul kills himself after being mortally wounded in battle, David mourns.

After Saul's death, David is anointed king of the southern tribe of Judah, and seven years later, he becomes king of a united Israel. Shortly thereafter, he makes Jerusalem his capital. He then goes on to defeat, or take as allies, the nations surrounding Israel.

Even David, however, is not perfect. In chapter eleven of *2 Samuel,* David commits adultery with a woman named Bathsheba. When God sends the prophet Nathan to call the king to account, David shows remorse. Nevertheless, David's personal problems multiply after this incident. This dark period culminates with an attempt by Absalom, one of his sons, to usurp the throne. In the end, however, David prevails, and the book ends with a tribute to Israel's greatest king.

Kings 1 and 2

The opening chapters of the first book of *Kings* describe the transfer of power from David to his son Solomon. Shortly after assuming the throne, Solomon asks God to grant him wisdom. Impressed that Solomon has not asked for riches or honor, God grants Solomon's request. As a bonus, the Lord gives the new king riches and honor as well. With a new era of peace and prosperity before him, Solomon undertakes the project that had been his father's dream: the building of a temple. Chapters six and seven describe the temple in detail, while chapter eight offers an account of the dedication ceremony. Word of Solomon's achievements spreads quickly, and foreign dignitaries—including the Queen of Sheba—soon come to see this legendary figure and his magnificent temple for themselves.

In chapter eleven, the story takes a sudden turn. Solomon, it seems, has one weakness—he is attracted to many exotic women. Eventually, his seven-hundred wives turn his heart toward other gods. Angered by Solomon's disobedience, God promises to undermine the kingdom. "For thy father's sake, I will not do it in thy days," He tells Solomon. "But I will rend it out of the hand of thy son."

After Solomon's death, the kingdom does indeed fall apart. First, two kingdoms are established: Judah in the south and Israel in the north. During the reign of King Ahab of Israel, there is renewed interest in Baal, a Canaanite god. The prophet Elijah performs a series of miracles to prove that Baal has no power, but it is clear that darker days are ahead.

The second book of *Kings* opens with Elijah's miraculous crossing of the Jordan. Shortly thereafter, the great prophet ascends into heaven. After Elijah's passing, the prophet Elisha takes his place, but the decline of the northern kingdom continues. Chapter seventeen describes the final takeover by the Assyrians.

A decade after the fall of the Northern Kingdom, the Assyrians attack King Hezekiah of Judah. The prophet Isaiah assures Hezekiah that Judah is safe for the time being. But he warns that Judah will eventually be overtaken by Babylon.

When King Hezekiah dies, he is replaced by Manasseh, his twelve-year-old son. Manasseh reigns for fifty-five years, but for much of that time he worships Baal "as Ahab of Israel had done."

True worship is restored when King Josiah assumes the throne, but thirty-one years later, in 609 B.C., Josiah is killed in battle. Shortly thereafter, the deportation of Jerusalem's citizens begins. Chapter twenty-five describes how "Nebuchadnezzar, king of Babylon, and all his army came against Jerusalem . . . and built a siege wall around it. After four months, "the city wall is broken through," and the remaining people are taken away into captivity.

Chronicles 1 and 2

The books of *Chronicles* are, for the most part, a repetition of the events described in earlier books. The first nine chapters of *1 Chronicles* are nothing but genealogies. The narrative begins in chapter ten with an account of King David's reign. The focus is somewhat different from *Samuel,* however, in that it emphasizes the rituals established by David and skips many of his military exploits.

The first nine chapters of *2 Chronicles* describe the reign of Solomon. From chapter ten on, the book tells the history of Israelites after Solomon's death. The book ends with the fall of Jerusalem.

Ezra

The focus of *Ezra* is the return of the exiles to the city of Jerusalem. It opens with the decree of Cyrus that those who wish to leave Babylon may do so. The rebuilding of the Temple is also authorized. In spite of Cyrus' decree, there is some opposition to the restoration. Nevertheless, under Cyrus' successor, Darius, the rebuilding of the Temple is completed.

Chapter seven describes the arrival of Ezra, an official who is sent by the Persian government to ensure adherence to Jewish law. The remainder of the book focuses on specific laws and rituals.

Nehemiah

The book of *Nehemiah* also describes the rebuilding of Jerusalem. It begins with an account of how Nehemiah, an exiled Jew, is sent back to Jerusalem to oversee the restoration. Like *Ezra*, the book of *Nehemiah* describes opposition to the rebuilding of the city on the part of lesser Persian officials. Nevertheless, the work goes on.

When work is finally complete, the people celebrate with the Feast of Tabernacles, also known as the Feast of Succoth. The celebration is followed by a mass confession and a review of the history of Israel, from Abraham onward. The remainder of the book, like Ezra, deals with legal matters—especially those involving contact with pagans.

Esther

Like *Ezra* and *Nehemiah,* the book of *Esther* describes events that took place under Persian rule. In particular, it tells the story of a Jewish maiden who became Queen of Xerxes and was instrumental in rescuing her compatriots from destruction.

Job

The book of *Job* tells the story of a righteous man who loses everything—his children, his health and his prosperity. The reason for his loss is explained in the first two chapters of the book. Satan questions Job's faith, and God agrees to test His "servant."

After Job suffers his losses, three friends come to comfort him. They are sympathetic but suggest that he must have done something to deserve his punishment. Job insists that he has done nothing wrong, and wonders aloud why he cannot plead directly with God.

Toward the end of the book, God answer's Job's call—but not for the purpose of explaining the events that have taken place. God's speech, which goes on for two chapters, focuses on the grandeur of Creation.

In the last chapter of the book, Job responds by acknowledging that he should not have questioned God's actions (or inaction). As a result, Job is blessed with greater prosperity than he had before.

Psalms

The book of *Psalms* contains one hundred and fifty separate poems. All of them converge on the theme of God's greatness, but they serve various purposes. Some are hymns of praise. Others are cries for help. Still others are offerings of thanksgiving.

The most famous Psalm, is number twenty-three, which reads, in part, "The Lord is my shepherd, I shall not want. . . He leads me in the paths of righteousness for His name's sake. Yea, though I walk through the valley of the shadow of death, I shall fear no evil."

Proverbs

Proverbs is a collection of sayings attributed to King Solomon. They deal with the proper conduct of life.

Specific topics include the hazards of expressing anger, the importance of diligence and the relative insignificance of material wealth.

Throughout the book, however, there is an emphasis on the value of wisdom. Indeed, you could say that the theme of the entire book is summed up in this line: "Happy is the man that findeth wisdom. . . For it is better than silver; and the gain thereof than fine gold. . . all things that thou canst desire are not to be compared unto it."

Ecclesiastes

Like *Proverbs,* this book is attributed to King Solomon—and it, too, emphasizes the importance of wisdom. The most famous passage is found in chapter three. It begins: "To everything there is a season, a time for every purpose under heaven: a time to be born, and a time to die. . . a time to kill and a time to heal. . ." Much of the rest of the book has a darker tone. According to the author, much of what man does on earth is "vanity" or "grasping for the wind."

The author concludes that life can have meaning only if we "Fear God and keep his commandments. . . For God will bring every work into judgment, including every secret thing, whether good or evil."

The Song of Solomon

Unlike the *Psalms,* which are monologues, this poem features several characters—specifically, a bride, a bridegroom, and a chorus. The poem's subject matter also sets it apart from other Biblical poetry. Here, the emphasis is not on God but on romantic love between man and woman. The man's speech in chapter four is representative of the poem as a whole. Searching for ways to express his admiration for his beloved, the man says, "Behold, thou art fair, my love! Thou hast doves' eyes. . . Thy lips are like a thread of scarlet. . . Thou hast ravished my heart." Some scholars have suggested that the poem may be read metaphorically, as a representation of God's love for His people.

Isaiah

The book of *Isaiah* is generally regarded as the most important book of prophecy. It is also one of the longest. It begins with a lament over the corruption of Judah in the eighth century B.C. It then warns that the people of Judah will suffer at the hands of their enemies as a result of their having turned their backs on God.

Nevertheless, the dominant tone of the book is one of hope. The author tells of the day when both Assyria and Babylon will fall, and a remnant of God's chosen people will return from exile. For Christians, the most pertinent parts of the book are those that appear to predict the coming of the Messiah. One such passage—written in the present tense, but presumably pertaining to the future—is found in chapter nine: "For unto us a child is born. . . And His name will be called. . . Prince of Peace. Of the increase of His government. . . there will be no end."

Jeremiah

The prophet Jeremiah is believed to have lived in the period just before the Babylonian Exile, and the book that bears his name reflects this crisis. Indeed, Jeremiah is often called the "weeping prophet" because the lamenting tone is so intense.

The beginning of the book calls on the people to repent, while the middle describes the last days of Jerusalem. The aftermath of Jerusalem's decline is also described. Finally, in chapter fifty-one, *Jeremiah* describes the utter destruction of Babylon.

Lamentations

Scholars believe that *Lamentations* was also written by Jeremiah, and it too deals with the fall of Jerusalem. Its style, however, is different from previous books. It consists of five separate poems about the people who have died at the hands of the Babylonians. Once again, though, a sense of hope and trust in God outweighs the author's anguish.

Ezekiel

Babylon besieged Israel for a number of years before the actual fall of Jerusalem in 587 or 586 B.C. During that period, many people were captured and forced to leave their homeland. Ezekiel was one of them, and this book was apparently written while he was living in exile. The book begins with a review of the sins of the people and the suggestion that the people must suffer as a result of those sins. But he too predicts that the nation will be restored.

Daniel

It is useful to divide this book into two parts. The first reads more like a story than a prophecy. Indeed, it contains one of the best-known and most popular tales in the Bible—the story of Daniel in the lion's den. The latter half of *Daniel* is often categorized as apocalyptic literature, and its imagery is very similar to that found in *The Revelation of St. John the Divine* at the end of the New Testament.

Hosea

The prophet Hosea is believed to have lived in the latter part of the eighth century B.C. In this book, he is told by God to marry a prostitute and to love her as God loves Israel—the idea being that Israel has become as corrupt as a harlot but that God will redeem her.

Joel

The focus of *Joel*—which consists of only three chapters—is the Day of Judgment. The opening chapter describes how the land has been devastated by a plague of locusts. In chapter two, God calls on the people to repent and promises that if they do the land will be restored. These descriptions of natural devastation and restoration are, of course, symbols of what will happen during God's final reckoning: sinners will be destroyed, but those who repent will be redeemed.

Amos

The prophet Amos is believed to have lived at about the same time as Joel and Hosea. He too focuses on the sins of the people and insists that there can be no redemption without repentance.

Obadiah

Obadiah, consisting of only a one chapter, is the shortest book in the Old Testament. Like many of the other prophetic books, however, it emphasizes that Israel will one day triumph. On that day, the children of Israel "Shall possess the land of the Canaanites. . . . And the kingdom shall be the Lord's."

Jonah

Like the first half of *Daniel,* the book of *Jonah* reads more like a story than a prophecy. At the opening of the book, God asks Jonah to travel to Nineveh where the people have sinned. Jonah is reluctant to accept God's command, and he attempts to escape on a ship. To punish him, God allows him to be swallowed up by a great fish. After three days, the fish releases Jonah, but the prophet is humbled by the experience. As a result, he agrees to travel to Nineveh. In the end, the people change their ways, and Jonah learns a lesson about God's mercy.

Micah

The style of *Micah* is similar to that of the major books of prophecy. Indeed, one passage in this book is identical to a passage in *Isaiah.* The emphasis here is on everything that God has done for His people and on the importance of adhering to God's Law.

Nahum

Like Jonah, the book of Nahum concerns itself with the city of Nineveh. Here, however, the emphasis is not on the city's redemption but on its destruction. The city did, indeed, fall, according to historians, around 612 B.C.

Habakkuk

Unlike most of the prophecies, which address the people on God's behalf, *Habakkuk* challenges God to explain why He allows His people to suffer at the hands of an unrighteous nation. God replies that the unrighteous will not go unpunished forever and that His people must have faith.

Zephaniah

The prophet Zephaniah is believed to have been a contemporary of Jeremiah, and his prophecy is a reflection of those troubled times before the fall of Jerusalem. Again, the book ends with an account of how God will redeem Israel.

Haggai

Haggai prophesied after the Babylonian Exile had ended. In this book, the prophet urges the people not to grieve over the devastation that Israel has suffered but to focus on the process of restoration. On the other hand, he is appalled that some of the people continue to live in relative luxury while the Temple has yet to be rebuilt.

Zechariah

Zechariah was associated with the prophet Haggai, but the imagery of this book is similar to that found in *Ezekiel* and *Daniel*. One passage, from chapter six, will suffice as an example: "Then I turned and raised my eyes and [beheld] four chariots coming from between two mountains. And the mountains were made of bronze. . . . Then I said to the angel of the Lord, 'What are these. . . ?' And the angel answered. . . 'These are four spirits of heaven. . . '"

Malachi

The focus of *Malachi* is corruption within the priesthood. In this way, it foreshadows the message of Jesus. It is therefore appropriate that it immediately precedes the New Testament.

The New Testament

The New Testament consists of four Gospels, focusing on the life, death and resurrection of Jesus; the *Acts of the Apostles,* which deals with the activities of Christ's followers after his crucifixion, and a series of letters written by St. Paul and other disciples.

The first three Gospels are called the "synoptic" Gospels because they have much in common with one another. There are, nevertheless, some key differences between *Matthew, Mark* and *Luke.*

Matthew

Matthew and *Luke* are the only two Gospels that describe the birth of Jesus, and to some extent these two accounts differ from one another. One noteworthy difference in *Matthew* is that the angel of the Lord appears to Joseph, rather than Mary, to announce the Virgin birth. Another is the visitation of wise men, rather than shepherds, to the scene of the Nativity. A third point of distinction is inclusion of the story of Joseph and Mary's flight to Egypt after the birth of Jesus. The story is not told in any of the other Gospels.

Chapters five through seven contain the Sermon on the Mount, the longest uninterrupted speech by Jesus in the entire New Testament. Included here are the Beatitudes and the Lord's Prayer.

Mark

Mark is the shortest of the Gospels. One major distinguishing feature is that it dispenses with Jesus' birth altogether and begins with the coming of John the Baptist. The other difference lies in the Gospel's overall focus. While *Matthew* emphasizes the words of Jesus, *Mark* seems more concerned with his deeds.

Luke

Luke contains a number of stories that are not found in any of the other Gospels, especially at the beginning of the book. These include: the annunciation to Mary; the story of John the Baptist's birth to Elizabeth; the adoration of the shepherds; the presentation of the infant Jesus in the Temple, and the account of Jesus, as a twelve-year-old, talking with scholars in Jerusalem. Yet another story that is unique to *Luke* comes toward the end of the book. After Jesus is crucified, he appears to two disciples on the road leading to the town of Emmaus. The disciples have dinner with the risen Lord but realize who he is only at the end of the meeting.

John

John is significantly different from the other three Gospels. Some of the specific differences include the story of the miracle at Cana; the story of the Good Shepherd, and the raising of Lazarus from the dead. Perhaps more important, however, is *John's* overall approach. Compared with the synoptic Gospels, *John* focuses on relatively few incidents in the life of Jesus. On the other hand, those that are included are explored indepth. Most of chapter six, for example, is devoted to the feeding of the five thousand. The other Gospels tell the story as well, but devote only a few lines to it.

Another important point of distinction is that *John* mentions the Last Supper only briefly. After the supper, on the other hand, great importance is given to a description of Jesus washing the feet of his disciples. This incident is not mentioned in the other Gospels.

Acts of the Apostles

Acts opens with a gathering of the apostles in Jerusalem after the death of Christ. A highlight of these early chapters is Peter's sermon in which he quotes the prophet Joel and urges everyone to "repent" and be "baptized in the name of Jesus. The book implies that such sermons were given on a daily basis, both in the temple and "from house to house," and that because of the apostles' work "the Lord added to the church daily. . ."

In time, Peter and John are arrested for their radical pronouncements, but they are subsequently freed, and they continue preaching that Jesus was the Messiah.

Among the apostles' opponents is a man named Saul. In an effort to locate followers of Christ and bring them back to Jerusalem, he travels to Damascus. On the way, however, he experiences a spontaneous conversion, and thereafter becomes the most ardent disciple of all. His name is changed to Paul, and he begins preaching throughout the Mediterranean world.

Paul is eventually arrested, but, because he is a Roman citizen he is granted a transfer to Rome. According to other sources, he was eventually executed there, but Acts does not record his death. The book ends simply by saying that Paul "dwelt there two whole years. . . teaching the things which concern the Lord Jesus."

Romans

Paul's letter to the Romans, written before he visited the city, emphasizes that Christ's message was intended for both Jews and gentiles and that all people must strive to love one another. The other important point in the letter is that faith guarantees deliverance from death.

1 Corinthians

In this letter to the church at Corinth, Paul calls for unity among followers of Christ, then goes on to discuss marriage, divorce and the importance of love in general. The letter contains what is perhaps the best-known passage in all of Paul's writings: "If I speak with the tongues of men and of angels, but have not love, I am but a sounding brass or a tinkling cymbal. And if I have the gift of prophecy, and understand all mysteries. . . but have not love, I am nothing. . . "

2 Corinthians

The overriding purpose of this follow-up letter to the church at Corinth appears to have been a defense of Paul's teachings. Other teachers had marred his reputation. But Paul makes it clear that he is not concerned with himself; he is interested only in distinguishing between the false teachings and the truths of which Christ spoke.

Galatians

Paul's determination to oppose false teachings is again reflected in this letter to the people of Galatia, a region in eastern Asia Minor. Specifically, Paul insists that Christians need not follow Jewish laws. What is essential is faith in Jesus.

Ephesians

This letter opens with a discussion of Christ's blessings, then moves on to specific instructions for the conduct of life. Chapter six, for example, emphasizes the importance of children obeying their parents, but, in turn, warns fathers not to provoke their children "to wrath."

Philippians

Paul had apparently been well-received by the people of Philippi, a city in northern Greece. Thus, in this letter, he devotes little space to a defense of his ministry. Instead, he simply encourages the community to stand firm in the face of persecution.

Colossians

Like *Ephesians,* this letter opens with reflections on the blessings of Christ, then proceeds to offer specific guidelines for everyday living. Not all of the passages are relevant to modern readers. There is, for example, a line urging bondservants to obey their masters. Nevertheless, much of the letter is timeless.

1 Thessalonians

Thessalonica was a city in northern Greece, not far from Philippi, and this letter is similar in tone to *Philippians.* It was designed to encourage followers of Christ and to reassure them that on "the day of the Lord"—i.e., the Day of Judgment—they would receive their eternal reward.

2 Thessalonians

The intent of this letter was to correct the notion that the day of the Lord had already arrived. After reassuring his readers, he urges them to live productive lives in keeping with the teachings of Christ.

Timothy 1 and 2

Timothy was one of Paul's assistants. The New Testament contains two letters attributed to Paul and addressed to Timothy. In the first letter, Paul uses his own experience as an example for others. He had been the worst of sinners and was forgiven; therefore, Christ's mercy must be "exceedingly abundant." He also discusses the running of the church and offers guidelines for ministers.

The second letter was written when Paul was in prison and quite possibly facing a death sentence. (The New Testament does not include an account of his death, but non-Biblical sources suggest that he was beheaded in Rome.) Paul urges Timothy to cling to his beliefs even though he will likely suffer for them.

Titus

Titus was another of Paul's assistants. Like *1 Timothy*, this letter urges Titus to continue spreading the message of Christ and to find others who can do the same. Additionally, he provides specific examples of sound doctrine and correct behavior.

Philemon

Philemon was a church leader whose slave, Onesimus, had run away. While Paul was in prison, he encountered Onesimus and converted him to Christianity. In this letter, Paul asks Philemon to forgive Onesimus and to treat him as a brother in Christ.

Hebrews

In The King James Version of the Bible this letter is attributed to Paul, but in more recent English translations no author is listed. In any event, the letter is quite different from the others in the New Testament. Like the Gospels, it includes numerous references to the Old Testament and states that Christ's life, death and resurrection fulfilled Old Testament prophecies.

James

Traditionally, this letter has been attributed to the brother of Jesus. Like many of Paul's letters—and the teachings of Jesus himself, as recorded in the Gospels—it emphasizes the importance of maintaining faith and loving one's neighbor.

Peter 1 and 2

The first of the two letters traditionally attributed to the apostle Peter echoes many of the other letters in the New Testament, emphasizing the importance of love, faith in Christ, and strength in the face of hostility and persecution.

Many scholars believe that the second letter was written by someone other than Peter. Nevertheless, it is presented as a letter from the apostle. It opens with a suggestion that his death is imminent then goes on to warn readers against "false prophets" and to emphasize that God's promises will be fulfilled.

John 1, 2 and 3

These letters have traditionally been attributed to the apostle John, and their style is quite similar to that of John's Gospel. In the first letter, John denounces non-believers, then urges the Christian community to unite in love for one another.

The second letter echoes the warning against false teachers, while the third addresses a community that had apparently rejected a teacher of truth.

Jude

Like James, Jude is thought to have been a brother of Jesus. In this letter, apparently written after many of the apostles had already been executed, he notes that false teachings have spread and urges followers to maintain their faith.

Revelation

The last book of the Bible is also a letter, but it is unlike any of those that come before it. Written by the apostle John to the seven churches of Asia Minor, the letter first evaluates each church, then proceeds to describe—in vivid detail—the coming Day of Judgment. Like the latter half of the book of Daniel, it contains a host of nightmarish images. In chapter six, for example, is the famous description of "a pale horse [whose rider] was Death—and Hades followed after him."

The overriding message, of course, is that sinners will face devastation while the faithful will be redeemed. After the corrupt cities of the world are destroyed, songs of victory are heard. Then, a new heaven and earth emerge.

Who's Who in the Bible

Aaron - The brother of Moses. Although Moses is a far more prominent figure in the Bible, Aaron plays a key role. In *Exodus 7:1*, God tells Moses, "Aaron shall be your prophet." Later, in *Exodus 28:1*, God identifies Aaron as the original member of the priesthood.

Abel - The second son of Adam and Eve. (See *Genesis 4:1-16*.) Abel is murdered by his brother, Cain, after God rejects Cain's offering but accepts a sacrifice from his brother.

Abraham (initially called Abram) - The first patriarch of the Hebrews, father of Isaac and wife of Sarah. In chapter 12 of the book of *Genesis,* God blesses Abram. From then on, his faith in God is unshakable. In Hebrew, his name means "father of a multitude."

Absalom - A son of King David. Driven by anger and ambition, Absalom attempts to take the throne from his father. (See *Samuel, 13-20.*)

Ahab - King of Israel in the middle of the ninth century B.C. Ahab had a reputation as a strong military and political leader. However, in the Bible he is an important figure principally because of his encounters with the prophet Elijah. (See *1 Kings 17-22*.)

Amos - A Hebrew prophet of the eighth century B.C.

Andrew - One of Jesus' twelve apostles and the brother of Simon Peter. (See *Matthew 4:18*.)

Augustus - Julius Caesar's grand-nephew and adopted heir. According to Luke, Augustus was the emperor of Rome at the time of Jesus' birth.

Baal - A Canaanite god. Opposition to the worship of Baal is a persistent theme of Israelite literature.

Baalzebub - Also, Beelzebub and Beel-zebul. A god worshipped by the Philistines. In the New Testament, Beelzebul is another name for the "prince of demons."

Barabbas - A prisoner held at the same time as Jesus, shortly before the Crucifixion.

Bartholomew - One of the twelve apostles. His name appears in all the lists of apostles but is not mentioned elsewhere.

Bathsheba - The woman with whom David commits adultery. (See *2 Samuel 11:1-4*.)

Belshazzar - The last king of Babylon. He gives a feast that is interrupted by the mysterious appearance of fingers writing on a wall.

Benjamin - Jacob's youngest son, born to Rachel.

Caiaphas - The high priest at the time of the trial of Jesus.

Cain - Adam and Eve's first son.

Daniel - According to the Old Testament book bearing his name, Daniel was a Jew who lived during the Babylonian Exile. He achieved recognition because of his ability to interpret dreams.

David - King of Israel from about 1010 to 970 B.C. David is considered the greatest monarch in the history of ancient Israel. The Gospels assert that Jesus was his direct descendant.

Delilah - A Philistine woman whom Samson loved. In exchange for a large sum of money, Delilah uncovers the secret of Samson's strength and reveals it to the Philistines.

Eli - A judge of Israel and the mentor and predecessor of Samuel.

Elijah - An Israelite prophet during the reign of King Ahab. (See *1 Kings 16:29-19:18*.)

Elisha - The successor of Elijah.

Elizabeth - The mother of John the Baptist and wife of Zechariah. (See *Luke 1:5-80*.) Like Abraham's wife, Sarah, and other prominent women of the Bible, Elizabeth had been "barren," or unable to bear children, but was singled out by God to become the mother of an important figure in Israel's history.

Esther - Wife of the Persian King Ahaseuerus, who ruled from India to Ethiopia in the fifth century B.C.

Ezekiel - A prophet taken to Babylon during the Exile by King Nebuchadnezzar. The Old Testament book that bears his name emphasizes Israel's repeated disobedience and rebellion.

Ezra - A priest and scribe. The Old Testament book that bears his name concerns the restoration of the Jewish community after the Exile.

Gabriel - One of the archangels. In *Luke 1:26 - 36*, he is the one who informs Mary that she will give birth to Jesus.

Gershom - Moses' eldest son.

Gideon - One of the great judges of Israel.

Goliath - A Philistine giant who vows that he will take on any Israelite in one-on-one combat. When David accepts the challenge, Goliath scoffs at the notion of fighting a young shepherd. David subsequently slays him by slinging a stone into his forehead.

Hagar - The Egyptian maidservant given to Abraham by Sarah. She became the mother of Abraham's first son, Ishmael.

Ham - One of Noah's sons.

Hannah - Mother of the prophet Samuel. Initially barren, Hannah vows that if she bears a son she will dedicate him to God.

Herod - The name of a family that provided governors of Palestine from about 55 B.C. until the end of the first century A.D. The Herod mentioned in the New Testament is thought to be Herod Antipas, son of Herod the Great.

Hiram - The king of Tyre and a contemporary of David and Solomon.

Hosea - A prophet active in the last years of the Northern Kingdom. The Old Testament book that bears his name echoes many of the themes of the other books of prophecy.

Isaac - The son of Abraham and Sarah, and the second patriarch of the ancient Hebrews. The word "Isaac" comes from the Hebrew word for "laughter," which was Sarah's reaction when she was informed that she was to bear a child at the age of ninety. Although Abraham loves Isaac, he accepts God's command to sacrifice the boy. At the last second, an angel stops the slaughter, telling Abraham that God is satisfied with his loyalty.

Isaiah - A prophet whose ministry lasted from approximately 740 to 701 B.C. The book that bears his name is the longest in the Old Testament. The first half of the book relates to the period of Assyrian conquest, while the second half deals with the Babylonian Exile and the final collapse of Babylon.

Ishmael - The son of Abraham by the Egyptian handmaiden Hagar (See *Genesis 16*.)

Jacob - The younger son of Isaac. His name was later changed to Israel. His twelve sons became the ancestors of the twelve tribes of Israel. (See *Genesis 25-35*.)

James - One of the twelve apostles and the brother of John. Jesus is also said to have had a brother named James, but he was not one of the twelve.

Japheth - One of Noah's three sons.

Jeremiah - A Judean prophet in the seventh and sixth centuries B.C. The Old Testament book that bears his name is noted for its heartfelt lamentations over the fall of Israel.

Jesse - The father of King David. (See *Samuel 16:3*.)

Jesus - See chapters seven through twelve.

Jethro - Moses' father-in-law.

Jezebel - A Phoenician princess who marries King Ahab of Israel.

Job - The main character in an Old Testament book by the same name. In the book, Job agonizes over the question of why God allows people to suffer undeservedly.

Joel - A common name in the Hebrew Bible, meaning "Yahweh is God." Also, the name of one of the prophetic books of the Old Testament.

John - One of the twelve apostles. Scholars are unsure as to whether John the Apostle was also the author of the *Gospel According to John*, the *Letters of John*, and the *Book of Revelation*.

John the Baptist - The forerunner of Jesus. (See sidebar, chapter seven.)

Jonah - An eighth-century B.C. prophet and the central character in an Old Testament book by the same name.

Jonathan - The son of King Saul and a close friend of David.

Joseph - The name of several characters in the Bible: 1) Jacob's favorite son. (See summary of *Gen-*

esis.); 2) The wife of Mary and, in the eyes of his contemporaries, the father of Jesus.

Joshua - As Moses' successor, Joshua leads the people of Israel into the Promised Land.

Josiah - King of Judah, who assumed the throne at the age of eight and reigned for thirty-one years.

Judah - The fourth son born to Jacob and his wife Leah.

Judas - The name of several characters in the Bible. The most famous is Judas Iscariot, the apostle who betrays Jesus. He is not to be confused with another apostle named Judas.

Levi - The third son of Jacob.

Luke - A companion of Paul and the presumed author of the third Gospel and the Acts of the Apostles.

Manasseh - King of Judah from 698 to 642 B.C. His fifty-five-year reign was the longest of any king of the house of David. According to the book of Kings, he was responsible for reintroducing pagan rituals.

Mark - The Acts of the Apostles and several New Testament letters mention Mark as a companion of Paul and Peter. Scholars do not know whether this Mark is also the author of the second Gospel.

Mary, the Virgin - See chapter seven.

Mary Magdalene - The most prominent of Jesus' female disciples and a primary witness to his death and resurrection.

Matthew - One of the original twelve apostles called by Jesus. Many scholars believe that the Gospel According to Matthew was written by someone other than Matthew the apostle.

Miriam - The sister of Moses. In *Exodus 15:20-21*, she is referred to as a prophetess.

Moab - Lot's son, born from an incestuous relationship with his elder daughter.

Moses - See chapters four through six.

Naomi - The mother-in-law of Ruth.

Nathan - A prophet in the court of David. After David commits adultery with Bathsheba (*2 Samuel 11*) God sends Nathan to rebuke the king.

Nebuchadnezzar - There were several kings named Nebuchadnezzar in ancient Mesopotamia. The king mentioned in the Bible is Nebuchadnezzar II who ruled Babylonia from 605 to 562 B.C.

Paul - The most effective missionary in the decades following the death of Christ. When he is introduced in the Acts of the Apostles, his name is Saul and he is vehemently opposed to followers of Christ. Subsequently, he experiences a spontaneous conversion.

Peter - One of the twelve apostles. His original name is Simon. The name Peter which means "rock" was given to him by Jesus.

Philip - One of the twelve apostles.

Pilate, Pontius - The Roman prefect, or governor, of Judea during the time of Jesus' public ministry and crucifixion. (See chapter eleven.)

Potiphar - Captain of the guard under the Pharaoh during the time of Joseph. Potiphar's initial impression of Joseph is favorable. Potiphar's wife tries unsuccessfully to seduce Joseph, then turns around and accuses him of trying to rape her.

Rachel - The more favored of the two wives of Jacob, and the mother of Joseph.

Rehohboam - Solomon's son and successor. He is the last king of the united monarchy, and the first king of Judah after the northern tribes rise up against him.

Reuben - Jacob's first son.

Ruth - The central character in the Old Testament book by the same name. Ruth is a Moabite woman who marries a well-to-do Israelite and gives birth to a child who eventually becomes the grandfather of King David.

Samuel - The last and greatest judge of the ancient Israelites. Samuel is important not only because of his own ministry but because he is the one who anoints King David. (See summary.)

Sarah - The wife of Abraham. Initially, she is called Sarai, but God changes her name. (See *Genesis 17:15*.) At the age of ninety, she gives birth to Isaac, who becomes the second great patriarch of the ancient Hebrews.

Saul - The first king of Israel, selected by God and anointed by Samuel. The early years of Saul's reign are successful, but, after making a rash vow to God, he falls from grace. His successor is David. Saul is also the original name of St. Paul. The reason for the name change is unclear, but it occurs some time after his conversion on the road to Damascus.

Seth - The third son of Adam, born after the death of Abel and the exile of Cain.

Simeon - The second son of Jacob and Leah. Simeon is perhaps best-known for his part in the massacre of the men of Shechem, which he undertook to avenge the rape of his sister, Dinah. (See *Genesis 34*.) A character name Simeon also plays a small but important role in the *Gospel According to Luke*. (See *2:25 - 35*.) The Holy Spirit has promised him that he would see the Messiah before he died. When Mary and Joseph present Jesus at the Temple, Simeon immediately recognizes him as the Messiah.

Simon - The original name of the Apostle Peter. *Luke* and *Acts* also mention an apostle named Simon the Zealot. Finally, both Matthew and Mark mention that Jesus has a brother named Simon.

Solomon - David's son and successor. During his forty-year reign, Solomon achieved fame as a ruler of great wisdom and as the builder of the elaborate Temple in Jerusalem.

Thaddaeus - One of the twelve apostles, according to *Matthew 10:3* and *Mark 3:18*.

Thomas - One of the twelve apostles. In the fourth Gospel, Thomas shows great courage and dedication in his willingness to accompany Jesus into Judea, even though it may mean death. He is best remembered, however, for a later incident. After Jesus' death, Thomas insists that he will not believe in the resurrection until he can see Jesus' scars and touch his wounds. The expression "doubting Thomas" comes from this story. (See *John 20:24-29*.)

Tiberius - The emperor of Rome during Jesus' public ministry. With the exception of *Luke 2:1*, all references to "Caesar" in the Gospels are references to Tiberius.

Timothy - A companion of St. Paul. In *1 Corinthians 4:17*, Paul refers to Timothy as "my beloved son [who is] faithful in the Lord." He is also the addressee of two of Paul's letters.

Zebedee - The fisherman father of two Apostles, James and John. Zebedee's wife was also a follower of Jesus. (See *Matthew 4:21-22* and *27:56.*)

Zechariah - There are no fewer than thirty people in the Bible with this name. Among them are: the father of John the Baptist; a king of Israel, who assumed the throne in 746 B.C.; a prophet who was active in Judah during the ninth century B.C.; and a prophet who ministered to the Israelites after the Babylonian Exile. The book of *Zechariah* in the Old Testament deals with the post-Exilic prophet.

Zephaniah - A prophet active during the seventh century B.C. The Old Testament book that bears his name deals, in large part, with the problem of idol-worship.

For Further Reading

The following books may be of interest to you if you wish to study the Bible and related topics in greater depth.

Achtemeier, Paul J., ed. *Harper Collins Bible Dictionary.* New York: HarperCollins, 1985, 1996. A comprehensive volume of 1200-plus pages, with entries on the people, places, terms and concepts mentioned in the Bible. Although it's called a "dictionary," many of its entries are actually full-length articles. (The entry on the Temple of Jerusalem, for example, is ten pages.)

Alter, Robert, and Frank Kermode, eds. *The Literary Guide to the Bible.* Cambridge, MA.: Belknap, 1987. Geared toward serious students who want to understand the Bible as literature.

Armstrong, Karen. *A History of God.* New York: Alfred A. Knopf, 1993. A fascinating look at how Judaism, Christianity and Islam have shaped humanity's conception of God. While the book is not about the Bible per se, it sheds light on many of the stories in the Old and New Testaments.

Bahat, Dan. *The Illustrated Atlas of Jerusalem.* New York: Simon and Schuster, 1990.

Bierlein, J.F. *Parallel Myths.* New York: Ballantine Books, 1994. Excerpts from mythical stories from around the world. For readers of the Bible, this book is especially useful because it puts the stories of Creation and the Flood into a broad cultural and historical perspective.

Bright, John. *A History of Israel.* Philadelphia: Westminster Press, 1981.

Friedman, Richard Elliot. *Who Wrote the Bible?* New York: HarperCollins, 1987, 1997. A well-researched, well-written effort to determine the authors of the Bible's various books.

Gabel, John B., and Charles B. Wheeler. *The Bible As Literature: An Introduction.* New York and Oxford: Oxford University Press, 1990. An excellent introduction to the Bible's various literary genres.

Gantt, Michael. *A Non-Churchgoer's Guide to the Bible.* Intercourse, PA: Good Books, 1995. An easy-to-read yet highly informative introduction. Gantt has something interesting to say about every book in the Old and New Testament.

Gomes, Peter J. *The Good Book: Reading the Bible with Mind and Heart.* New York: William Morrow and Company, 1996. Gomes, minister of Harvard University's Memorial Church, explores the Bible's relevancy in the modern world. Includes chapters on suffering, temptation, evil, and joy.

Keller, Werner. *The Bible as History.* New York: Bantam Books, 1974. Originally published in Germany, this landmark book explores the historical foundations of the Scriptures. Includes chapters on the Flood, the Hebrew patriarchs, the battle for the Promised Land, Jesus, and other topics.

Metzger, Bruce M., and Michael D. Coogan, eds. *The Oxford Companion to the Bible.* Oxford and New York: Oxford University Press, 1993. Contains alphabetical listings, of varying lengths, on important people, places, events and themes of the Bible.

Porter, J.R. *The Illustrated Guide to the Bible.* New York: Oxford University Press, 1995. An engaging and informative introduction to the Bible. Porter looks at the Scriptures from literary, historical and theological perspectives.

Reader's Digest. *The Bible Through the Ages: From Papyrus to CD-ROM, the Story of How the Bible Came to Be.* Pleasantville, NY: The Reader's Digest Association. Reader's Digest has published numerous books on the Bible. All are informative, user-friendly and nicely illustrated.

Rogerson, John. *Atlas of the Bible.* New York: Facts on File, 1985. In addition to maps, this useful volume contains photographs and illustrations on everything from plants mentioned in the Bible to Biblical warfare.

Romer, John. *Testament: The Bible and History.* New York: Henry Holt, 1988. Romer describes the process by which the Old and New Testaments came into being and explains how and why the Bible has survived to this day.

Taylor, Mark D. *The Complete Book of Bible Literacy.* Wheaton, IL: Tyndale, 1992. Contains more than 1,200 entries, which deal not only with people and places but with phrases and individual stories. In addition to an entry on "Daniel," for example, there is an entry for "Daniel in the Lion's Den." The book's entertainment value is enhanced by fourteen self-scoring quizzes.

Vermes, Geza. *The Complete Dead Sea Scrolls in English.* New York: Allen Lane/The Penguin Press, 1962, 1997.

Visotzky, Burton L. *Reading the Book: Making the Bible a Timeless Text.* New York: Schocken Books, 1991.

Index

Picture Credits

All art courtesy of Art Resource, except for the following:

Page 21: Adam and Eve, by Lucas Cranach, the Elder, Norton Simon Art Foundation.

Page 33: Expulsion from the Garden of Eden, by Thomas Cole, Museum of Fine Arts, Boston.

Pages 54-5: Noah's Sacrifice, by Joseph Anton Koch, Städelscheles Kunstinstitut, Frankfurt/Artothek.

Page 65: The Sacrifice of Isaac, by Caravaggio, Scala/Art Resource.

Page 69: Jacob Receiving the Tunic of Joseph, by Diego Velazquez, Escorial, Madrid.

Pages 74-5: Joseph Recognized by His Brethren, by Baron Franáoise Pascal Gerard, Angers Musee des Beaux Arts.

Page 85: The Finding of Moses by Pharaoh's Daughter, by Sir Lawrence Alma-Tadema, Bridgeman Art Library.

Pages 98-9: The Departure of the Israelites, by David Roberts, Birmingham City Museum and Art Gallery.

Page 110: Moses Strikes the Rock, by James Jacques Joseph Tissot, Jewish Museum/Art Resource.

Page 112: The Gathering of Manna in the Desert, by Nicolas Poussin, Erich Lessing/Art Resource.

Page 121: Moses Destroying the Golden Calf, by Andrea Celesti, Cameraphoto/Art Resource.

Page 142: St. Joseph and the Infant Christ, by Giovanni Battista Gualli, Norton Simon Art Foundation.

Page 143: Madonna and Child, by Giovanni Bellini, Metropolitan Museum of Art.

Page 145: Finding the Savior in the Temple, by William Holman Hunt, Birmingham City Art Museum.

Page 152: The Baptism of Christ, by Piero della Francesca, National Gallery, London.

Page 175: The Marriage at Cana, by Master of the Catholic Kings, National Gallery of Art, Washington D.C.

Page 176: The Transfiguration, by Giovanni Bellini; , Scala/Art Resource.

Page 179: St. Peter, by Leonardo da Vinci, Erich Lessing/Art Resource.

Page 190: Christ and the Virgin, by Michelangelo Buonarotti, Scala/Art Resource.

Page 194: The Institution of the Eucharist, by Nicolas Poussin, Scala/Art Resource

Page 196: Head of Christ, by Leonardo da Vinci, Alinari/Art Resource.

Page 201: Christ Washing Peter's Feet, by Ford Madox Brown, The Tate Gallery, London.

Pages 204-5: The Sacrament of the Last Supper, by Salvador Dali, The National Gallery of Art, Washington, D.C.

Page 212: Agony in the Garden, by Andrea Mantegna, National Gallery, London.

Page 215: The Denial of Peter, by Gerrit van Honthorst, Minneapolis Institute of Fine Arts.

Page 231: Christ on the Cross, by Eugene Delacroix, National Gallery, London.

Page 237: The Angel Opening the Sepulchre of Christ, by Albert Cuyp, Museum of Fine Arts, Budapest/Artothek.

Page 240: The Incredulity of St. Thomas, by Guercino, Scala/Art Resource.

Page 241: Noli me Tangere, by Antonio Correggio, Bridgeman/Art Resource.

Pages 242-3: The Supper at Emmaus, by Caravaggio, Scala/Art Resource.